MEN'S SCRIPTURE
MEMORY GUIDE

Learning God's Word from Genesis to Revelation

ED STRAUSS

BARBOUR PUBLISHING

Previously released as *A Genesis-to-Revelation Scripture Memory Guide*

ISBN 979-8-89151-085-2

Published by Barbour Publishing, Inc., 1810 Barbour Drive, Uhrichsville, Ohio 44683, www.barbourbooks.com

Our mission is to inspire the world with the life-changing message of the Bible.

Member of the Evangelical Christian Publishers Association

Printed in the United States of America.

CONTENTS

INTRODUCTION

Commanded to Memorize the Word

It might seem strange, but many modern Christian men have never seriously considered memorizing verses or passages from the Bible. They think it's a lot of work, and they don't see how doing so would benefit them in any practical way. But in ancient Israel, there was an entirely different mindset.

God said, "These words which I command you today shall be in your heart. You shall teach them diligently to your children" (Deuteronomy 6:6–7 NKJV) and "Therefore shall ye lay up these my words in your heart and in your soul" (Deuteronomy 11:18 KJV).

As a result, Jewish children in Jesus' day memorized many scriptures. For boys, this began at five years of age in the village *bet ha-sefer* ("house of the book"). They spent half a day, six days a week learning, and since practicing writing by copying out the sacred scriptures wasn't considered proper, they spent the bulk of their day committing portions from the Torah (the five books of the Law) to memory. The Jewish historian Josephus boasted, "The result then of our thorough grounding in the laws from the first dawn of intelligence is that we have them, as it were, engraven on our souls."

At age ten, boys graduated to the *bet talmud* ("house of learning"), where they began memorizing the Mishnah, the Oral Law, and learned how to interpret the Torah. A few young Jewish men went on to become disciples of a rabbi, as Peter and Andrew did with John the Baptist and later with Jesus. But their education began and was founded upon committing many passages from God's Word to memory—and many continued memorizing scriptures in their later years.

Scripture memorization isn't just for children. Adults can and should memorize Bible verses too! You may object that you have a poor memory and find memorization difficult, but this book will break it down and make it simple. It's time for you to claim the many benefits of plugging your mind and spirit into God's Word.

In this book, we focus on 144 of the most basic, important scriptures that Christians need to memorize—and explain why they're vital to your spiritual health—plus we supply an additional 49 verses that you might also wish to memorize.

1

DAILY BIBLE READING

Memorizing key passages from the Bible is vital both to anchor you in Christ, the Son of the living God, and to establish you firmly in Christian doctrine. But simple memorization can never replace a faithful, prayerful study of God's Word in daily Bible reading.

Without a broader knowledge of the overall scriptures, Bible memorization won't be as illuminating as it could be. Some errant religious groups insist that all members memorize the same verses to indoctrinate them in their peculiar beliefs, while ignoring Bible passages that give a wider and sometimes conflicting message. They memorize verses that answer common objections to convince you that they're right when they come knocking at your door. It can be very impressive to have a person quote scriptures quickly and confidently in answer to your queries. It gives the impression that they know the Word of God well. . .and that they have the truth. But they've often only memorized a few key scriptures—while ignoring surrounding passages that supply much-needed context.

Those attending authentic Bible-believing churches must also know verses in context. Second Timothy 2:15 (KJV) exhorts, "Study to shew thyself approved unto God, a workman that needeth not to be ashamed, rightly dividing the word of truth." A zealous young man once told me that he was going to ask God to do a miracle on his teeth. He said that he was claiming the Bible's promise "I also have given you cleanness of teeth." He hadn't paid attention to the rest of the verse, or he would've known that God was talking about judging Israel's sins with a severe famine. The entire passage reads, "And I also have given you cleanness of teeth in all your cities, and want of bread in all your places: yet have ye not returned unto me, saith the LORD" (Amos 4:6 KJV).

You must not only read your Bible every day, but also meditate on it and study it. You must crack open the dry bones to get at the rich marrow (see Psalm 63:5). It's a good idea to buy a Bible handbook so you can look up the historical, religious, social, and economic context of what you're reading. Don't just be satisfied with getting the general gist of a passage. Learn exactly what it's talking about. As the Bible says, "They read distinctly from the book, in the Law of God; and they gave the sense, and helped them to understand the reading" (Nehemiah 8:8 NKJV). If you read the New International Version, Zondervan has put out the helpful *NIV Study Bible*. If you read the King James Version, Barbour Publishing has published the handy *KJV Study Bible*.

I have found that daily Bible reading has an added benefit: Besides the many verses and their references that I made a deliberate effort to commit to memory, I have semi-memorized hundreds of other verses that I can quote (sometimes verbatim), simply because I've read and pondered them so many times during my daily devotions. Often when praying for a needed answer, a phrase from one of these verses I've so frequently read comes to my mind. For example, one time I was facing a financial emergency and could see no way to come up with the needed funds in time. I felt like throwing up my hands in despair. Then, totally out of the blue, the Holy Spirit impressed this passage on my mind: "The children of Ephraim, being armed, and carrying bows, turned back in the day of battle" (Psalm 78:9 KJV). The Lord was reproving me for giving up when I had the resources to handle the emergency.

I'd never memorized that verse, and frankly, it was so obscure that I didn't recall even having read it before. But I must have read it for the Spirit to be able to bring it to my memory. . . verbatim. And the instant that verse came to mind, I remembered a way I *could* raise the cash—so I tried it and it worked! This was in clear fulfillment of Jesus' promise, "But the Helper, the Holy Spirit. . .will teach you all things, and bring to your remembrance all things that I said to you" (John 14:26 NKJV).

It would be difficult to overemphasize the importance of daily Bible reading—and this doesn't mean just hastily racing your eyes over a couple of chapters every morning to fulfill a reading quota, but meditating on the passages you plainly understand, reading them slowly to let their meaning sink in. It also means pondering and mulling over things you don't understand and researching them in Bible study books.

2

BENEFITS OF MEMORIZING SCRIPTURE

You receive many benefits from memorizing scripture. The following are the more important ones:

1—A Solid Foundation

Two good reasons you should memorize God's Word are so you may be "rooted and built up in Him *and* established in the faith" (Colossians 2:7 NKJV, emphasis added). The first reason, so that you can be "rooted and built up in [Christ]," is the most important, but the second reason, so that you can be "established in the faith," is also crucial.

Knowing the Word of God strengthens your personal connection and your relationship with Christ. Jesus said, "Those who accept my commandments and obey them are the ones who love me" (John 14:21 NLT), so you can't claim you love Jesus if you make no effort to obey Him. And here's the catch: It's very difficult to obey His commands if you don't have a clear idea of what He actually said and commanded.

Paul instructed, "Let the word of Christ dwell in you richly in all wisdom" (Colossians 3:16 NKJV). You need to be strongly connected to Christ, and focus on Him and His simple, powerful message—to love God and your fellow man (Mark 12:30–31). You must be "rooted and grounded in love" (Ephesians 3:17 KJV).

Paul wanted Timothy to be "a good minister of Jesus Christ, nourished in the words of faith and of the good doctrine which [he had] carefully followed" (1 Timothy 4:6 NKJV). It's important to have a clear idea of basic "good doctrine" and to know what Jesus *said* and *didn't say*. A young Christian man once told a friend and me that all religions were valid paths to God, and to prove his point, he asked us, "After all, doesn't the Bible say that all religions are equal?" "*Noooo*," we informed him. "It doesn't" (see John 14:6).

Although you don't want to go overboard on doctrine and use verses like sledgehammers to drive your point home to others, Paul is clear that you need to be informed as to what is good, wholesome doctrine so that you can carefully follow it.

2—Guiding Decision-Making

Since the reason for knowing the words of Jesus is so that you can obey them, it's clear that you should know the Word of God well enough that it can guide you in making your decisions. A wonderful thing about memorizing Bible verses is that they're then available to inform your choices. Jesus said, "The Helper, the Holy Spirit. . .will teach you all things, and remind you of all that I said to you" (John 14:26 NASB). But before the Holy Spirit can remind you of Jesus' words, you need to impress them on your memory first.

Too many Christians make serious life decisions based on little more than a faint, positive impression, or on whether the word *yes* or *no* forms in their mind. They assume that these thoughts are God's Spirit speaking, when it's often as not just their own mind. Don't get me wrong: I believe God *can* communicate directly to individual believers, but if you're really honest, you'll have to admit that more than a few decisions made based upon such faint impressions never worked out (see Ezekiel 13:6–7).

To make solid, good decisions, you need to study God's Word. Then He can truly speak to you: "The unfolding of Your words gives light; it gives understanding to the simple" (Psalm 119:130 NASB).

3—Avoiding Sin

God said, "The word is very near you, in your mouth and in your heart, that you may *do* it" (Deuteronomy 30:14 NKJV, emphasis added). And Psalm 119:11 (NKJV) says, "Your word I have hidden in my heart, that I might not sin against You." Hiding God's Word in your heart means more than simply memorizing it. It implies absorbing His instructions into the core of your being with the clear intent to love and obey them.

Jesus repeatedly quoted the Word of God to Satan when he tempted Him to disobey God (see Matthew 4:1–10). To every one of the devil's temptations, Jesus answered, "It is written," then quoted a passage verbatim from God's Word. The scriptures Jesus had memorized as an inquisitive youngster in the *bet ha-sefer* of Nazareth—and in the years following, as a young man—sprang from His memory to His tongue, and He used them to defeat the evil one's deceptions.

And you shouldn't wait until you're in the middle of fiery temptations to try to use the Word to fight them. You can ponder verses to strengthen yourself beforehand and devise strategies to avoid being tempted in the first place. For example, Job 31:1 (NIV) says, "I made a covenant with my eyes not to look lustfully at a young woman." This is a clear reminder that you also need to set strong defenses in place well before temptation can spring out to ambush you.

4—Dispelling Confusion

God's Word is the standard by which we measure all truth and error. Isaiah bluntly declared, when speaking of Old Testament scripture, "To the law and to the testimony! If they do not speak according to this word, it is because there is no light in them" (Isaiah 8:20 NKJV). You must also obey "the word of Christ" (Colossians 3:16 NASB), because Jesus is the promised Prophet of Deuteronomy 18. "Moses said, 'The Lord God will raise up for you a prophet like me from your countrymen; to Him you shall listen to everything He says to you. And it shall be that every soul that does not listen to that prophet shall be utterly destroyed from among the people'" (Acts 3:22–23 NASB).

It pays to know God's Word so that you'll "no longer be children, tossed to and fro and carried about with every wind of doctrine" (Ephesians 4:14 NKJV). If you don't have a clear idea what the Bible says, then deceivers can easily mislead you. Many Christians have been led into mistaken doctrine—and into blatantly false doctrine—through a lack of knowing the Bible. Jesus told the religious leaders of His day, "You are in error because you do not know the Scriptures or the power of God" (Matthew 22:29 NIV). Don't let this be you.

5—Having a Ready Response

Another important reason for memorizing scripture is that it enables you to share your faith more effectively. This is why Christians memorize basic salvation scriptures—Romans 3:23; 6:23; John 3:36; etc.—and quote them when they encounter a truth seeker. They don't even need to have a Bible handy to explain what it says. You can quote verses while pouring cement or doing dishes, or at other times when it's not even a good idea to be holding a Bible. This fulfills 1 Peter 3:15 (NIV), which advises, "Always be prepared to give an answer to everyone who asks you to give the reason for the hope that you have."

From the prodigious amounts of scripture the apostles spontaneously quoted, both in open-air settings and in synagogues, it's clear that they had spent a considerable amount of time committing scripture to memory (see Acts 2:16–21, 25–28; 4:25–26; 7:42–43, 49–50; 13:33–35, 41; etc.). It certainly paid off for them, and it can for you too.

6—Taking the Shield of Faith

In Ephesians 6:16 (NKJV), Paul instructs believers, "Above all, taking the shield of faith with which you will be able to quench all the fiery darts of the wicked one." Romans 10:17 (NKJV) says, "So then faith comes by hearing, and hearing by the word of God," so the Word of God generates the power that this shield uses to protect you.

When you're trying to go to sleep at night but find yourself worrying about your finances, your children, your health, or any number of other issues, you quickly realize how well spent was the time you invested in memorizing promises from the Bible. When you find that you can quote God's Word accurately and with authority during times of utter darkness and severe spiritual testing, when you can "quench all the fiery darts of the wicked one" and dispel fear, then you will feel truly grateful for time you invested in scripture memorization.

7—Gaining Spiritual Authority

Memorizing Bible verses can add real strength and authority when you make desperately needed requests in prayer.

When Jacob was returning to Canaan after dwelling for twenty years in Haran, he was in a truly desperate situation: "Jacob said, 'God of my father Abraham and God of my father Isaac, LORD, who said to me, "Return to your country and to your relatives, and I will make you prosper" . . . Save me, please, from the hand of my brother, from the hand of Esau; for I fear him, that he will come and attack me and the mothers with the children. For You said, "I will assuredly make you prosper and make your descendants as the sand of the sea, which is too great to be counted"'" (Genesis 32:9, 11–12 NASB).

God had made promises to Jacob down through the years, and when he faced tremendous danger, Jacob quoted two of those promises back to Him. Jacob had repeated these promises to himself so many times over the years that they were etched on his memory—and they gave him the strength he needed in his darkest hour, in his time of severe testing.

3

TIPS FOR MEMORIZATION

Here are some practical tips for committing Bible verses to memory. Use the following techniques to write God's Word on your heart:

1. Whenever you choose to memorize verses that really interest you or that answer questions you've been wrestling with—or that meet a pressing emotional or spiritual need in your life—you're highly motivated to remember them. For example, I memorized Philippians 4:7 (KJV) one day when I was reeling from a great disappointment. It promises, "And the peace of God, which passeth all understanding, shall keep your hearts and minds through Christ Jesus." I've never forgotten it after all these years and have frequently quoted it during times of worry or sorrow.

   Likewise, I memorized 2 Thessalonians 3:3 (NIV) during a period when I felt under heavy attack by the devil. This verse promises, "But the Lord is faithful, and he will strengthen you and protect you from the evil one." I quote it every time my spirit is troubled and needs reassuring, and it quickly brings me peace.

2. In this book, I suggest 144 verses worth memorizing, even if you don't feel passionate about them at this time or feel an urgent need to remember them. But like getting daily exercise or eating healthy, you know memorizing scripture is

something you need to do faithfully. The good news is, you can still infuse the memory process with emotion.

Remind yourself that it's the very Word of God, and as Jesus said, "The words that I speak to you are *spirit*, and they are *life*" (John 6:63 NKJV, emphasis added). That's something to get excited about! Also, the prophet Jeremiah declared, "Thy words were found, and I did eat them; and thy word was unto me the joy and rejoicing of mine heart: for I am called by thy name, O LORD God of hosts" (Jeremiah 15:16 KJV). Seek to feel the text, remind yourself that it will change you, and think deeply about its power and meaning. This will engage your emotions.

3. Read each verse out loud several times, emphasizing the stresses and pauses in the sentences that help bring out its meaning. Hearing yourself speak the Word adds an audio dimension to the visual. And don't simply drone on. Speak the words with emotion. Abraham Lincoln was famous for his prodigious memory, and reading aloud was his favorite technique for remembering important information. It nearly drove his law partner, William Herndon, crazy when Lincoln read aloud newspaper articles, legal books, and other material that he wished to remember. But as Lincoln explained, reading things out loud was like etching something on metal. It never faded.

4. Repeat each new verse twenty times in the morning, ten times in midday, and another ten times in the evening before bedtime—or even more often if you find that extra repetition is required to etch God's Word on your heart. Do this often enough and you will have the verse memorized by the end of the day.

   Remember to quote the Bible reference after the verse

every time, as it's very helpful to memorize the reference as well. You need to know exactly where the verse is in case someone questions whether the Bible actually says that or should you need to look it up to discuss its context.

5. On the first day, write the verse out ten times. Physically writing the words out is an excellent visual aid.

6. Be sure to also write your new memory verses on small flash cards. (You can buy 3-by-5-inch flash cards in stationery stores or dollar stores.) Then keep these cards together in a small box so you can review them. Review your newest memory verses faithfully every day at first. Later on, just review them once a week. Review all your older memory verses once a month, or as needed.

7. Use your new memory verses in your prayers, if they fit. Pray that God will not only help you remember them but also help you understand and apply these verses to your life.

8. Tape a printed copy of the day's verse on your wall, on your computer monitor, to your bathroom mirror, on your fridge, or in any other place where you'll see it often or several times a day. Type out the passage on your tablet or in your phone where it's easily accessible when you're away from home.

9. Whatever techniques you use in memorizing Bible verses, repeat the verses many times. Repeat, repeat, repeat! Quote the verse over and over until saying it accurately comes naturally and easily.

4

WHAT JESUS MEMORIZED

Jesus not only memorized passages from the Torah (the five books of Moses), as all Jewish boys were required to do, but He memorized passages from all over the Psalms and the prophets—verses in Bible books from Genesis to Malachi.

The Gospels record Jesus quoting more than two dozen Old Testament passages. They are Genesis 1:27; 2:24; Exodus 3:6; 20:12–16; Deuteronomy 6:5; 8:3; 6:13, 16; Leviticus 19:18; Psalm 8:2; 22:1; 31:5; 78:2; 82:6; 110:1; 118:22–23, 26; Isaiah 6:9–10; 29:13; 66:24; Hosea 6:6; 10:8; Micah 7:6; Zechariah 13:7; and Malachi 3:1. No doubt, Jesus memorized and quoted many more verses that aren't recorded in the Gospels. The following passage demonstrates that:

"And then He said to them, 'You. . .slow of heart to believe in all that the prophets have spoken! Was it not necessary for the Christ to suffer these things and to come into His glory?' Then beginning with Moses and with *all the Prophets*, He explained to them the things written about Himself in *all the Scriptures*" (Luke 24:25–27 NASB, emphasis added).

Jesus was on the road to Emmaus with two of His disciples and didn't have a copy of the scriptures to read from. So He was quoting passages from "all the Scriptures" that He had committed to memory as a young man.

Memorizing these passages also allowed Jesus to be fully aware of what His future held (Mark 10:32–34), helped Him to be mentally and spiritually prepared for all that He would suffer, and enabled Him to later teach these fulfilled prophecies to His disciples. Memorizing key scriptures strengthened Jesus. When the mob seized Him at the garden of Gethsemane, Peter drew a sword to defend Him, but Jesus ordered him to put away his weapon, asking, "How then would the Scriptures be fulfilled, which say that it must happen this way?" (Matthew 26:54 NASB).

You too will benefit from memorizing verses from the length and the breadth of God's Word. The memory verses in this book come from every book of the Bible. They can apply to your life situations today.

5

AN OVERVIEW OF THE BIBLE

GENESIS: Genesis is the book of beginnings, and it opens with the creation of the heavens and the earth. It goes on to describe how God promised Abraham, Jacob, and Isaac that He'd give their descendants the land of Canaan. It later tells of Jacob and his family moving down to Egypt during a famine.

EXODUS: Exodus recounts the story of the Israelites as slaves in Egypt, and it tells how God sent ten plagues to persuade Pharaoh to let them go free. Moses led the Israelites through the Red Sea and into the desert. They stopped at Mount Sinai, received the Law, and built the Tabernacle (Tent of Meeting).

LEVITICUS: This book contains many religious rules and ceremonial laws—hence its name *Leviticus*, after the priestly tribe of Levi. The Levites performed blood sacrifices, received tithes, and served God in the Tabernacle. The book of Leviticus also describes the many annual festivals.

NUMBERS: This book receives its name because in it, God twice tells Moses to perform a census to number the men of military age. Numbers describes the Israelites' journeys through the Sinai Desert, their murmuring and rebellions, and major events in their journey to the border of Canaan.

Deuteronomy: When the Israelites were in Moab, east of Canaan, after the older, disobedient generation had died out, Moses renewed God's covenant with the younger generation and reviewed their history. This book contains repeats of stories from Exodus and Numbers.

Joshua: This book describes how Joshua (who had been appointed to lead the Israelites after the death of Moses) marched the Israelites into Canaan, and it tells of their six-year war to conquer the Promised Land. When Joshua retired, he pointed out that much land remained to be conquered.

Judges: This book describes how, over a period of hundreds of years, God raised up judges to rule Israel. The Israelites went through continual cycles of disobedience to God and idol worship, oppression at the hands of their enemies, and then deliverance through judges and anointed military leaders.

Ruth: This short book describes the lives of Naomi, an Israelite widow, and Ruth, her Moabite daughter-in-law. Ruth followed Naomi back to Bethlehem, where she gleaned during the barley harvest; Ruth then married Boaz, a wealthy landowner, and became an ancestor of David.

1 Samuel: This book describes Israel's history from the prophet Samuel to Saul, Israel's first king. It tells the story of Saul's wars and disobediences, the rise of David, and Saul's persecution of David. This book ends with the Philistines defeating Israel's army and records the death of Saul and his sons.

2 Samuel: This book begins with David becoming king over Judah, then over all Israel, and then details his many wars and the tumultuous events of his forty-year reign. It describes David's virtues as well as his sins and then ends with his death and his son Solomon becoming king.

1 Kings: This book (written during the Jewish exile in Babylon) describes the history of Israel under its kings Solomon and Rehoboam, its division into two kingdoms, and the many events and wars of the later kings of Judah and Israel, up until the time of the prophets Elijah and Elisha.

2 Kings: This book begins with Elijah's ascension to heaven and continues the history of the kings of Judah and Israel, up to the Assyrian invasion and deportation of the people of the northern kingdom, Israel. It then describes the Babylonian invasion and exile of the southern kingdom, Judah.

1 Chronicles: Written after the Jews were restored to their land during the Persian Empire, 1 Chronicles is largely a retelling of David's reign over Israel. The Chronicles focus on God's temple, so this first book describes the preparations David made for its building.

2 Chronicles: This book describes Solomon building the temple, then after his reign, focuses almost exclusively on the kingdom of Judah up until the Babylonian exile—giving much attention to the temple and the priesthood. It makes almost no mention of the northern kingdom.

Ezra: The book of Ezra tells the story of the Jews returning to their land after the Exile and their struggles to rebuild the temple despite much opposition. It details Ezra the scribe coming to Jerusalem to teach the Jews, and explains that he stopped the Jews from intermarrying with foreign women.

Nehemiah: This is the story of Nehemiah, the Persian king's cupbearer, and it describes the king allowing him to travel to Jerusalem to rebuild its walls. Nehemiah bravely led the work despite much opposition, and the city was once again safe from enemy attacks.

Esther: This book describes Esther, a beautiful Jewish woman who became the queen of Persia. After her cousin Mordecai refused to bow to Haman, an enemy of his people, Haman ordered the extermination of all Jews, but Esther interceded with the king and spared her people.

Job: This is the story of Job, a righteous man, and how Satan demanded that God cause him severe suffering to test him. Job's friends came to comfort him, but instead condemned him for his supposed sins. In the end, God set the record straight and restored Job's fortunes.

Psalms: This lengthy book is a collection of many prophetic psalms and poetic writings. Some are songs of praise, and some are poems exalting God, His acts, and His Word. Some of the psalms are laments and complaints. David wrote many of these psalms, but several other writers also contributed.

Proverbs: The proverbs are wise sayings and biblical principles that were written largely by Solomon, though other wise people wrote a few of them. The proverbs aren't necessarily ironclad promises to claim in all circumstances but are astute, general observations about life situations.

Ecclesiastes: Solomon also wrote this book of wise, melancholy life observations. Many people think he wrote this "despairing" book after he fell away from God, but Ecclesiastes 12:10, 13 indicates that Solomon had returned to the Lord before its writing.

Song of Solomon: Also titled the Song of Songs, this book contains vivid poetry extolling emotional and physical love within marriage. The Jews believe it symbolically describes God's love for Israel; Christians believe it's a parable of Christ's love for His bride, the church.

Isaiah: Isaiah is the first book of the Major Prophets. Isaiah the man is believed to have been of royal blood, and he lived in Jerusalem during the difficult days of the Assyrian Empire. His book contains many comforting promises, as well as prophecies of the coming Messiah and kingdom of God.

Jeremiah: Jeremiah prophesied that God was sending the Babylonians to conquer idolatrous Judah, and he counseled the Jews to submit to God and live. But the Jews clung to their idols and kept rebelling. As a result, the Babylonians destroyed Jerusalem and took the people into exile.

Lamentations: This book of laments, written by Jeremiah, shows why he's called "the weeping prophet." Jerusalem had suffered a siege and famine and then fell to the Babylonians, and Jeremiah confessed that all this happened because God's people had stubbornly disobeyed Him.

Ezekiel: Ezekiel was a Levite who had been taken as an exile to Babylon. Once there, he began receiving warning prophecies from God. Ezekiel performed a number of skits to get his message across and gave a lengthy prophecy about a new temple that God said would be built.

Daniel: Daniel is the last of the Major Prophets. He was taken to Babylon as a youth, and while there, because of his courage and wisdom, he became King Nebuchadnezzar's top counselor. He had a series of prophetic visions about empires down through history and about end-time events.

Hosea: This book is the first of the Minor Prophets. It describes how God told Hosea to marry an adulterous woman and be faithful to her, despite her wanderings. This was to portray God's love for His covenant people, even though they had been unfaithful to Him. Hosea obeyed, and even his three children's names were prophetic messages.

Joel: The prophet Joel gave a message to Israel after a massive locust plague, coupled with a severe drought, had devastated the land. Joel compared the locusts to the vast, invading army that God would send to punish His people. But Joel also promised God would send restoration.

Amos: Amos was a farm laborer from Tekoa, a village near Bethlehem, just before the rise of the Assyrians. Because the Jews were prospering, they believed that they were pleasing God. Amos warned them, however, that God was about to judge them for their social injustices.

Obadiah: This very short book contains a prophecy about the Babylonians' destruction of Edom. Obadiah 1–9 is almost identical to Jeremiah 49:7–16, and this likely means that Obadiah preached Jeremiah's message and recorded it in his own writings.

Jonah: Jonah lived in Israel just before the rise of the Assyrians, just as the Israelites experienced a time of great prosperity (see Amos). God told Jonah to warn the Assyrians of impending judgment, but Jonah disobeyed, ran from God, was swallowed by a great fish, then repented and went to Nineveh to warn them.

Micah: This book contains the oracles of Micah, a prophet from southern Judah who lived during the days of Isaiah, when the Assyrian Empire was rising in power. Micah warned the Israelites that God would judge them, but he also promised their deliverance and future glory.

Nahum: In this book, the prophet Nahum warned that God was about to judge Nineveh and the Assyrian Empire because of their idolatry, cruelty, and oppression. This was welcome news because the Assyrians had destroyed northern Israel and had attacked and oppressed Judah.

Habakkuk: The prophet who wrote this book lived at the same time as Jeremiah, during Judah's dying days, under the shadow of the Babylonians. Habakkuk is famous for questioning why God allowed the people of Judah to continuously do evil and then used evil pagans to judge them.

Zephaniah: This prophet was a descendant of King Hezekiah and lived after the reign of evil King Manasseh but before good King Josiah began his religious reforms. Zephaniah probably knew Jeremiah, and like him, he warned that God was going to send judgment on Judah.

Haggai: Haggai lived during the days of the Persian Empire, when the Jewish exiles returned to Judah. They were afraid to rebuild the temple, so he prophesied, encouraging them to proceed. God spoke through him, promising: "From this day on I will bless you" (Haggai 2:19 NIV).

Zechariah: This prophet was also a priest, and he lived at the same time as Haggai, whom he joined in encouraging the Jews to rebuild. Zechariah continued to prophesy long after Haggai, however. His main message was one of encouragement. He made several Messianic prophecies as well.

Malachi: Malachi wrote the final book in the Old Testament, and he was the last of the Minor Prophets. Malachi prophesied in Nehemiah's day, rebuking the people for their hypocrisy and lethargy. They constantly questioned Malachi's charges, for which he repeatedly rebuked them.

Matthew: Levi (Matthew) was a tax collector who became an apostle of Jesus. He wrote his Gospel for the Jews of Israel and the Greek-speaking Jews of the Diaspora. It contains many parables and fulfilled prophecies proving that Jesus was the long-awaited Messiah.

Mark: Mark (Barnabas' cousin) wrote this Gospel under the influence of Peter. It's short and action-packed, full of colorful language, and constantly uses the word *immediately*. It's believed that Mark had a Roman audience in mind. This was possibly the first Gospel to be written.

Luke: Luke was a Gentile and a physician, and he compiled and wrote this Gospel under the influence of Paul. Luke had the Greeks largely in mind when he wrote his Gospel; the Greeks idealized "the perfect man," and Luke demonstrated that this is exactly what Jesus was.

John: John (the "beloved disciple") was one of Jesus' original twelve apostles, and his was the last of the Gospels written; thus, he didn't cover the same ground the other three had but gave many new details and stories. This is a deeply spiritual account, and its preface declares boldly that Jesus is God.

ACTS: The Acts of the Apostles is part 2 of Luke's work, and it takes up where his Gospel left off. It describes the history of the early church, including the miracles, doctrinal issues, and the exploits of Peter and Paul—who preached the gospel throughout much of the Roman Empire.

ROMANS: This lengthy epistle of Paul (written from Corinth before Paul sailed for Jerusalem and then Rome) succinctly explains the basics of the Christian faith and is considered a theological masterpiece. Romans is one of the most-quoted books in the Bible.

1 CORINTHIANS: Paul wrote his first epistle to the church in Corinth when he was in Ephesus. In it, he deals with their problems and doctrinal issues—sectarian divisions, sexual immorality, lawsuits, spiritual gifts, and the resurrection. It also contains the renowned Love Chapter (chapter 13).

2 CORINTHIANS: False apostles had infiltrated the church in Corinth and questioned Paul's authority, so he wrote this second epistle, telling the Corinthians the proofs of his apostleship. He then urged them to finish collecting their relief funds for the poor Christians of Jerusalem.

GALATIANS: This is one of Paul's earliest letters. Some legalistic Jewish believers were insisting that Gentile Christians had to keep the Law of Moses to be saved. In this short, powerful epistle, Paul insisted that Jews and Gentiles alike were saved by faith in the grace of God alone.

EPHESIANS: Paul wrote this epistle to Ephesus in AD 60 while under house arrest in Rome. This letter doesn't address any specific issue; rather, it contains Paul's prayers and encouragement for the

Ephesians to more deeply understand God's grace, purpose, and love for the church.

Philippians: Paul likely wrote this epistle to the church in Philippi in AD 61 while still under house arrest in Rome. He encouraged the Philippians to stand strong despite persecution. In chapter 2, he described Christ's great humility although "being in very nature God" (verse 6 NIV).

Colossians: Paul wrote this short epistle to the church in Colossae at the same time as his epistle to the Ephesians. Paul warned against two heresies—one: Jewish legalism, and two: a teaching that was the beginnings of a heresy known as Gnosticism. Paul emphasized the divine nature and preeminence of Christ.

1 Thessalonians: This is probably Paul's earliest epistle, written about AD 51. Paul had been forced to flee Thessalonica before he grounded new converts in the faith, so he wrote this letter to teach them Christian truths and to encourage them to withstand the persecution they suffered.

2 Thessalonians: Paul wrote this epistle about six months after his first letter to Thessalonica, again encouraging them to stand strong during persecution. Paul also taught them the signs to look for in the days before the second coming of Christ.

1 Timothy: Paul wrote this epistle to Timothy about AD 65, after he had been rearrested and was being held in the Mamertine prison in Rome. In it, Paul advised Timothy, a young pastor in Ephesus, about the duties of overseers and deacons, about widows, materialism, and other personal matters.

2 Timothy: This was Paul's final epistle, written shortly before his execution in AD 66–67. He urged Timothy to come from Ephesus to Rome. Many coworkers had abandoned Paul, and the churches of Asia Minor had turned against him, but Paul maintained a victorious attitude.

Titus: Paul wrote this epistle in Ephesus in about AD 63. Paul had been released from house arrest in Rome and had evangelized Spain. Returning to the East, he and Titus worked in Crete, where Paul left him to organize the churches. Paul wrote Titus to advise him in his work.

Philemon: Paul wrote this epistle at the same time as his letter to Colossae, and had Onesimus (a runaway slave who had become a Christian) deliver it to Philemon, his former master. Paul asked Philemon to forgive Onesimus for stealing money and leaving, and he requested that Philemon grant his freedom.

Hebrews: Scholars aren't certain who wrote this dissertation about Christ becoming an eternal priest in the Order of Melchizedek, having fulfilled the Law by offering one final blood sacrifice. Chapter 11 (Heroes of the Faith) and chapter 12 (on God's chastisement) are powerful classics.

James: James, Jesus' brother, wrote this epistle to Jewish Christians of the Diaspora before AD 50. In it, James spoke forcefully about the importance of faith-inspired works, social justice versus selfishness, living the Royal Law by loving others, and guarding your tongue.

1 Peter: The apostle Peter wrote this letter about AD 65 with the aid of Silas (1 Peter 5:12). In it, Peter talks about living for God, marital relationships, slaves and masters, and enduring persecution. Peter's discussions here are similar to the speeches he gave in the book of Acts.

2 Peter: Peter wrote his second epistle about AD 66–67. Its Greek isn't as polished as that of his first epistle, probably because Peter wrote this letter without the help of Silas, his Greek scribe. In 2 Peter 3:15–16 Peter referred to Paul's writings as "Scripture."

1 John: The apostle John penned this epistle about AD 90, after writing his Gospel. It contains a series of powerful messages on God, His love, and eternal life. It also speaks out against the Gnostic heresy, which was developing and spreading among churches at this time.

2 John: The apostle John jotted this brief epistle about AD 90 to an unnamed Christian lady who hosted and aided traveling teachers. John cautioned her to use discernment, to be sure the ministers she received taught orthodox doctrine and weren't Gnostic deceivers.

3 John: A proud, controlling church leader named Diotrephes refused to receive traveling teachers John had sent and was excommunicating Christians who did receive them. John wrote this epistle about AD 90 to address the problem.

Jude: Jude, the brother of Jesus, wrote this brief letter around AD 65. Its message is very similar to that of 2 Peter 2:1–10, and most Bible scholars believe that Peter borrowed from Jude's message. Jude speaks against those who turned God's grace into sexual permissiveness.

Revelation: This book of apocalyptic visions was written by the apostle John in AD 96, after Domitian's persecution of Christians. John recorded it to encourage the disciples of his day not to succumb to emperor worship and to warn believers of all ages about difficult times to come.

6

DIFFERENT TRANSLATIONS AND TEXTS

Many people prefer the King James Version of the Bible for its beauty and elegance, and for the fact that it's a very literal translation, faithful to the Hebrew and Greek texts upon which it's based. Others, however, point out that the KJV is four hundred years old and that its use of *thee* and *thou* (and other archaic terms) puts it out of touch with modern readers and makes it difficult to understand. They argue that the NIV is a thoroughly modern translation and that the balance it strikes between clarity and literal equivalency makes it a better translation.

But the differences between the KJV and the NIV go deeper than translation approaches. The underlying Hebrew and Greek texts upon which they're based also frequently differ from each other. Compare, for example, the wording of Matthew 5:44 in the KJV and the NIV. The KJV states: "But I say unto you, Love your enemies, bless them that curse you, do good to them that hate you, and pray for them which despitefully use you, and persecute you," but the NIV only has the words: "But I tell you, love your enemies and pray for those who persecute you."

It should be noted that the parallel passage in Luke 6:27–28 contains the exact same full Greek text in both the KJV and the NIV. So Jesus definitely said the fuller message, even if it wasn't included in Matthew 5:44 in the NIV. But this brings up the question:

Which Greek manuscripts are the most accurate New Testament texts? To answer this question, we must first note that most New Testament manuscripts belong to one of three textual families. The differences between these textual groups cause both scholars and laypeople to advocate one above another. This dispute goes back sixteen centuries.

The Old Latin translations, including the Latin Vulgate, are based upon a text that has come to be called the Western Text. When Jerome translated the Vulgate around AD 400, he also had access to the Byzantine Text (of Lucian of Antioch) and the Alexandrian Text (of Hesychius of Egypt), but he spoke disparagingly of both. Thus the Western Text, through Jerome's Latin translation, dominated Western Europe from about AD 400 until the 1500s.

During this time, however, Christians of the Greek-speaking Byzantine Empire continued using the Byzantine Text. After Constantinople fell in 1453, some of these manuscripts were brought to the West, where a scholar named Erasmus compiled them into one text. Martin Luther's New Testament and the King James Version are based upon this compiled text (later called the Textus Receptus—the Received Text). This Greek text dominated the Christian world for 450 years.

Then in the late 1800s, scholars discovered the Codex Vaticanus and Codex Sinaiticus, copies made at a very early date. These both contained examples of the Alexandrian Text, though they frequently disagreed even with each other. Once again, however, the "new" readings were compiled into one text, which scholars believe is now the most accurate version. Today, most Bible translations are based on the Alexandrian Text.

So which Greek text is actually most accurate? While some people, like Jerome, exclusively favor one text and speak disparagingly of the others, many scholars believe that all these texts have an important part to contribute. It's worth noting that there are far more differences in our modern Bibles due to translation styles than to differences in the original Greek texts.

It's frequently claimed that the KJV is superior because it stresses the deity of Christ, whereas the NIV either omits such mentions or downplays them. This is sometimes the case. But in three places, the opposite is true—the NIV emphasizes the deity of Christ while the KJV passes over it in silence. In the KJV, John 1:18 says, "No man hath seen God at any time; the only begotten Son, which is in the bosom of the Father, he hath declared him." But the NIV boldly states, "No one has ever seen God, but the one and only Son, who is himself God and is in closest relationship with the Father, has made him known."

In the KJV, Titus 2:13 says, "Looking for that blessed hope, and the glorious appearing of the great God and our Saviour Jesus Christ." It sounds like it's talking about two persons, God the Father and Jesus His Son. But the NIV states, "We wait for the blessed hope—the appearing of the glory of our great God and Savior, Jesus Christ." It says clearly that Jesus is not only the "Savior" but also "our great God." Which translation is most accurate? According to Granville Sharp's rule of Greek grammar (which is invariably true in Greek literature), the NIV is more accurate in this case.

It's also more accurate in 2 Peter 1:1. There, the KJV refers to "God and our Saviour Jesus Christ" but the NIV translates it "our God and Savior Jesus Christ." Again, the NIV declares the deity of Christ, whereas the KJV does not. So the Greek texts for the KJV and the NIV both stress Christ's deity.

Whichever translation and Greek textual family you prefer, be aware that other translations and the textual families they belong to have rich traditions and solid reasons to trust in them. So although you may prefer one translation above the others, there's no reason to disparage the others.

6

144 MEMORY VERSES

Salvation

GOD'S INCOMPARABLE GLORY

You may be used to thinking of "sin" as a horrible, dark, filthy deed—something that therefore doesn't fit you—but the Greek word frequently translated in the New Testament as "sin" is *hamartema*, and it simply means "to miss the mark." You might not think of yourself as a degraded sinner crawling through the gutters, but you can admit that you've missed the mark many times, can't you? You can admit that you're not perfect like God, right? This is what Paul meant when he wrote:

For all have sinned, and come short of the glory of God.
Romans 3:23 KJV

For all have sinned and fall short of the glory of God.
Romans 3:23 NIV

God is glorious beyond all comparison, and Paul wrote of Him as a God "who alone has immortality, dwelling in unapproachable light, whom no man has seen or can see, to whom be honor and everlasting power" (1 Timothy 6:16 NKJV). Finite, fallible human beings can't begin to compare to the infinite, surpassingly glorious God of heaven. So of course you fall short of the glory of God—far short.

THE END RESULT OF SIN

Even after you come to terms with the fact that you're a sinner, your reaction might be, "So I'm a sinner. So what? I'm only human. No one is perfect, after all." Sin may seem trivial since, after all, everybody sins—but the end result is not trivial. Sin adds up and in the end pays you deadly wages. The final paycheck is death to your body and spirit.

For the wages of sin is death; but the gift of God is eternal life through Jesus Christ our Lord.
Romans 6:23 KJV

For the wages of sin is death, but the gift of God is eternal life in Christ Jesus our Lord.
Romans 6:23 NIV

When you're finally at the point where you admit that you're a sinner, then you must realize that "the wages of sin is death." Romans 6:23 first gives the bad news, but then it gives good news. Many people presume that they're "good" and look forward to being rewarded for it, but the Bible states that if you received what you deserved, you'd receive death. But God offers you eternal life as a gift of unmerited grace.

THE IMMENSE LOVE OF GOD

The verse below is perhaps the best-known verse in the Bible—and for good reason. It captures the very heart of the scriptures. The key thought is that God so very deeply loved humanity that He gave the most precious thing He had—His one and only Son, who was, as the Nicene Creed states, "Light of Light, very God of very God, begotten, not made." He gave Jesus, who had dwelt for eternity "in the bosom of the Father" (John 1:18 NKJV), as a sacrifice for your sin.

For God so loved the world, that he gave his only begotten Son, that whosoever believeth in him should not perish, but have everlasting life.
JOHN 3:16 KJV

"For God so loved the world that he gave his one and only Son, that whoever believes in him shall not perish but have eternal life."
JOHN 3:16 NIV

John 3:16 contains a simple, very powerful truth: All that is required for you to be saved is to cry out to God, to reach out and take hold of Christ, and put your trust in Him. When you do that, He guarantees He will save you: "For 'whoever calls on the name of the LORD shall be saved'" (Romans 10:13 NKJV).

FILLED WITH GOD'S LIFE

Jesus described salvation as being "born again" or "born of the Spirit" (John 3:7–8 NKJV). What did He mean? Well, before you encountered Christ, your spirit was dead, alienated from the life of God (Ephesians 2:12). But when the Spirit of God's Son entered your heart, He completely renewed you and gave you spiritual life. In that instant, you were born of the Spirit and were transformed into a son of God.

And because ye are sons, God hath sent forth the Spirit of his Son into your hearts, crying, Abba, Father.
GALATIANS 4:6 KJV

Because you are his sons, God sent the Spirit of his Son into our hearts, the Spirit who calls out, "Abba, Father."
GALATIANS 4:6 NIV

God sent the Spirit of His Son into your heart, and Jesus gives eternal life to every human spirit He touches (John 17:2). Paul wrote, "He who is joined to the Lord is one spirit with Him" (1 Corinthians 6:17 NKJV), so when the Spirit of Christ entered and became one with your spirit, His light and power swept through your entire being and infused you with life.

STEPS OF SALVATION

Salvation is a simple process: You must have faith in Christ and must confess Him to others—not necessarily to everyone, if doing so would needlessly endanger you, but certainly to those who know you best.

That if thou shalt confess with thy mouth the Lord Jesus, and shalt believe in thine heart that God hath raised him from the dead, thou shalt be saved. For with the heart man believeth unto righteousness; and with the mouth confession is made unto salvation.
Romans 10:9–10 KJV

If you declare with your mouth, "Jesus is Lord," and believe in your heart that God raised him from the dead, you will be saved. For it is with your heart that you believe and are justified, and it is with your mouth that you profess your faith and are saved.
Romans 10:9–10 NIV

Some people wonder, "Why am I required to give voice to my faith in Christ? Doesn't God look at my heart? Isn't faith all that's necessary?" Well, the Bible states, "I believed, therefore have I spoken" (Psalm 116:10 KJV), and Jesus tells us that "the mouth speaks what the heart is full of" (Luke 6:45 NIV).

SAVED BY GRACE

You often hear that we're "saved by grace." What does this mean? According to the dictionary, the word *grace* is (a) "a favor rendered by one who need not do so"; (b) "the free and unmerited favor of God"; (c) "divine favor bestowed freely on people, as in granting redemption from sin." And what does "favor"—used in all three definitions—mean? The word favor is "an act of kindness beyond what is due." Now you understand what Paul meant when he wrote:

For by grace are ye saved through faith; and that not of yourselves:
it is the gift of God: not of works, lest any man should boast.
Ephesians 2:8–9 KJV

For it is by grace you have been saved, through faith—
and this is not from yourselves, it is the gift of God—
not by works, so that no one can boast.
Ephesians 2:8–9 NIV

As this verse explains, salvation is a gift. You can't boast that you worked for this gift and earned it. If you could, it would be wages God was obliged to pay you. It wouldn't be a gift (Romans 4:4). That's what the Bible means when it says, "Not by works of righteousness which we have done, but according to his mercy he saved us" (Titus 3:5 KJV).

YOU HAVE ETERNAL LIFE NOW

If the Spirit of Christ dwells in you, you don't need to hope that God will one day allow you to open His gift of salvation and receive eternal life. It's yours here and now! John reassures you that your name is already written in the Book of Life, your paperwork is approved, and you're a citizen of heaven, free to enter the heavenly realm (Philippians 3:20; 4:3).

He that hath the Son hath life; and he that hath not the Son of God hath not life. These things have I written unto you that believe on the name of the Son of God; that ye may know that ye have eternal life.

1 JOHN 5:12–13 KJV

Whoever has the Son has life; whoever does not have the Son of God does not have life. I write these things to you who believe in the name of the Son of God so that you may know that you have eternal life.

1 JOHN 5:12–13 NIV

The Amplified Bible states, "Now faith is the assurance (title deed, confirmation) of things hoped for (divinely guaranteed)" (Hebrews 11:1). You already possess the title deed to your heavenly inheritance.

INVITING JESUS IN

Some two thousand years ago, Jesus and His disciples ate their final meal together—a traditional Passover supper consisting of lamb, bread, herbs, dip, and wine. This meal served as an annual reminder of the Lord saving His people in Egypt. Jesus told His disciples, "I have been very eager to eat this Passover meal with you" (Luke 22:15 NLT). He had not only looked forward to this time, but very eagerly desired it. Even today He says:

Behold, I stand at the door, and knock: if any man hear my voice, and open the door, I will come in to him, and will sup with him, and he with me.
REVELATION 3:20 KJV

"Here I am! I stand at the door and knock. If anyone hears my voice and opens the door, I will come in and eat with that person, and they with me."
REVELATION 3:20 NIV

Jesus still eagerly desires fellowship with believers, so be sure to spend time with Him daily, feasting on His Word and meditating on Him. This verse is also frequently applied to the initial salvation experience—you hearing Jesus knocking on your heart, opening the door, and allowing Him to enter. Have you invited Jesus in?

WALKING IN NEWNESS OF LIFE

When the Spirit of Christ enters your life, He changes your entire outlook—often radically. You become a new person. Indeed, many of your former habits are gone instantaneously. But, as you have surely discovered, the transformation isn't complete on Day 1. For the process to come to completion, you need to do as this verse says and live "in Christ"—not just for one day but for your entire life, day in and day out.

Therefore if any man be in Christ, he is a new creature: old things are passed away; behold, all things are become new.
2 CORINTHIANS 5:17 KJV

Therefore, if anyone is in Christ, the new creation has come: The old has gone, the new is here!
2 CORINTHIANS 5:17 NIV

That is why, although "the new is here," Paul says that it's your responsibility to "walk in newness of life" (Romans 6:4 KJV). And as 2 Corinthians 4:16 (NASB) explains, we are "being renewed day by day." Following Jesus and daily being transformed into His image is a lifelong process that requires a great deal of patience and endurance.

GOOD WORKS AND SALVATION

Paul repeatedly emphasized that "by grace you have been saved. . .not as a result of works" (Ephesians 2:8–9 NASB), so some people conclude that James contradicts Paul when he stresses the need for works. But though you aren't saved by doing good deeds, once you're saved, visible works are proof of the inner transformation.

And Jesus commanded, "Let your light so shine before men, that they may see your good works, and glorify your Father which is in heaven" (Matthew 5:16 KJV). James's statement is in keeping with this. He says:

For as the body without the spirit is dead,
so faith without works is dead also.
James 2:26 KJV

As the body without the spirit is dead,
so faith without deeds is dead.
James 2:26 NIV

Like James, Paul warned against those who claim to have faith but have no good works: "They profess that they know God; but in works they deny him, being. . .disobedient, and unto every good work reprobate" (Titus 1:16 KJV). There's no contradiction between James and Paul.

GOD TRANSFORMS YOU

God promised His people, "I will give you a new heart and put a new spirit within you; and I will remove the heart of stone from your flesh and give you a heart of flesh" (Ezekiel 36:26 NASB). In the next verse, God stated a beautiful promise, saying exactly what He'd do:

> *And I will put my spirit within you, and cause you to walk in my statutes, and ye shall keep my judgments, and do them.*
> EZEKIEL 36:27 KJV

> *"And I will put my Spirit in you and move you to follow my decrees and be careful to keep my laws."*
> EZEKIEL 36:27 NIV

God sends the Spirit of His Son into your heart when you believe in Him (Galatians 4:6), and His Spirit moves you to walk in His love and follow Him. It's not you alone trying to live a Christian life, but the Spirit of God moving your heart. Paul wrote, "For we are. . .created in Christ Jesus for good works, which God prepared beforehand that we should walk in them" (Ephesians 2:10 NKJV).

GOD WILL FINISH THE JOB

Many Christians think it's all well and fine that Jesus saves them, but they harbor the worry that once He saves them, from then on the ball is forever in their court, and it's their job to keep themselves saved. This thought, if true, would make anyone's hair turn gray. But God's Word offers comfort:

> *Being confident of this very thing, that he which hath begun a good work in you will perform it until the day of Jesus Christ.*
> PHILIPPIANS 1:6 KJV

> *Being confident of this, that he who began a good work in you will carry it on to completion until the day of Christ Jesus.*
> PHILIPPIANS 1:6 NIV

"The day of Jesus Christ" refers to the time of His second coming, when He returns to earth to judge the wicked and to save His children from them. So in this passage, God promises not only to initially save you but to continue performing His miraculous work until it's complete—until the very day Jesus returns. Not only can you believe this, you can be *confident* of it.

GOD'S KEEPING POWER

You were once separated from God. To lose your salvation, you'd have to be once again separated from Him. But the Bible says that nothing has the power to do that. Jesus said, "I give unto them eternal life; and they shall never perish. . .and no man is able to pluck them out of my Father's hand" (John 10:28–29 KJV). This is why Paul confidently stated:

> *For I am persuaded, that neither death, nor life, nor angels, nor principalities, nor powers, nor things present, nor things to come, nor height, nor depth, nor any other creature, shall be able to separate us from the love of God, which is in Christ Jesus our Lord.*
> Romans 8:38–39 KJV

> *For I am convinced that neither death nor life, neither angels nor demons, neither the present nor the future, nor any powers, neither height nor depth, nor anything else in all creation, will be able to separate us from the love of God that is in Christ Jesus our Lord.*
> Romans 8:38–39 NIV

This promise should comfort you greatly when the enemy tells you that God is fed up with you and has cast you out. Stand firm in your faith in God's unchanging love.

TREASURE IN HEAVEN

Jesus specifically commanded believers to focus on spiritual realities and to set their hearts on heaven, not earth. If you do that, you'll be willing to invest your time and energy in heavenly endeavors instead of merely seeking earthly riches.

Lay not up for yourselves treasures upon earth, where moth and rust doth corrupt, and where thieves break through and steal: but lay up for yourselves treasures in heaven, where neither moth nor rust doth corrupt, and where thieves do not break through nor steal: for where your treasure is, there will your heart be also.
MATTHEW 6:19–21 KJV

"Do not store up for yourselves treasures on earth, where moths and vermin destroy, and where thieves break in and steal. But store up for yourselves treasures in heaven, where moths and vermin do not destroy, and where thieves do not break in and steal. For where your treasure is, there your heart will be also."
MATTHEW 6:19–21 NIV

You still should set money aside for retirement. And don't give all your life savings to missions and have nothing left to sustain you in your old age. But you should also invest heavily in spiritual things.

THE FATHER OF FAITH

One night, when Abraham—at that time called Abram—was nearly one hundred years old, God told him that a son who would come from his own physical body would be his heir. God then said, "Now look toward the heavens, and count the stars, if you are able to count them." Then God told Abraham, "So shall your descendants be" (Genesis 15:5 NASB). The Bible then says this about Abraham's response to God's promise:

And he believed in the LORD;
and he counted it to him for righteousness.
GENESIS 15:6 KJV

Abram believed the LORD,
and he credited it to him as righteousness.
GENESIS 15:6 NIV

Abraham could have doubted. After all, at one hundred years of age, his body was as good as dead, and Sarah's womb had failed to conceive even when she was young and healthy. How much more so now that she was ninety? (See Romans 4:19.) But Abraham was convinced that God had spoken, so he believed. For this act of trust—apart from any good deeds Abraham had ever done—God counted him as a righteous man. Furthermore, Abraham became known as "the father of all who believe" (Romans 4:11 NASB).

GOD FORGIVES ALL SIN

Many a time, when you're overwhelmed with guilt over your sins and wonder if God can forgive you, quoting the verse below will turn the tide. Notice that it says God "is faithful and just" to forgive you. God is not only faithful to forgive, but He's just in so doing. You might have expected it to say that He's merciful to forgive, but it states that He's just. Why? Because He has promised to forgive you, and He keeps His promises.

If we confess our sins, he is faithful and just to forgive us our sins, and to cleanse us from all unrighteousness.
1 JOHN 1:9 KJV

If we confess our sins, he is faithful and just and will forgive us our sins and purify us from all unrighteousness.
1 JOHN 1:9 NIV

God will forgive your sins, cleanse you, and make you innocent in His sight. There is a condition, however. Proverbs 28:13 (NKJV) states, "He who covers his sins will not prosper, but whoever confesses and forsakes them will have mercy." You have to not only confess your sins but wholeheartedly repent of them.

GOD REMOVES SIN'S STAINS

In ancient times, to ensure that the expensive color crimson remained permanently in a garment, the cloth was dyed twice. The Hebrew word used in the verse below literally means "double-dyed." But God promises that even though His people were double-dyed with sin, He'd so thoroughly remove the stain that they'd be white like wool. Isaiah 1:15, 21 refers to the people as murderers having hands stained red with blood, but God promised to remove even *that* sin.

Come now, and let us reason together, saith the Lord:
though your sins be as scarlet, they shall be as white as snow;
though they be red like crimson, they shall be as wool.
Isaiah 1:18 KJV

"Come now, let us settle the matter," says the Lord. "Though
your sins are like scarlet, they shall be as white as snow;
though they are red as crimson, they shall be like wool."
Isaiah 1:18 NIV

God invites you to draw near to Him and reason with Him. He's completely reasonable and open to explaining matters. So don't be stubborn and unreasonable. Come talk with God today.

FORGIVING AS GOD FORGAVE

Jesus took all your sins on Himself on the cross and paid the penalty for them. As a result, God counts your debts to Him "paid in full." He then requests that you show the same mercy He's shown you to your fellow man. In fact, He says, "If you forgive those who sin against you, your heavenly Father will forgive you. But if you refuse to forgive others, your Father will not forgive your sins" (Matthew 6:14–15 NLT). Paul underscored this kind of forgiveness when he wrote:

And be ye kind one to another, tenderhearted, forgiving one another, even as God for Christ's sake hath forgiven you.
Ephesians 4:32 KJV

Be kind and compassionate to one another, forgiving each other, just as in Christ God forgave you.
Ephesians 4:32 NIV

To be willing to forgive others, you must have a tender heart. You must have compassion. The word *compassion* means "a feeling of deep pity and concern for another, accompanied by a strong desire to alleviate their suffering." When you truly know God, you realize the fundamental truth that "God is love" (1 John 4:8 KJV), and His love can move you to acts of compassion.

JESUS HAS COMPASSION ON YOU

You may be aware of your weaknesses and bemoan the fact that you often succumb to temptation. You may realize that you frequently waver when confronted by sin, and you may think that a perfect, holy God despises you. But Jesus knows how you feel. Though He is God's Son, He too was tempted to sin (see Matthew 4:1–10). So He understands you and has great compassion on you.

For we have not an high priest which cannot be touched
with the feeling of our infirmities; but was in all
points tempted like as we are, yet without sin.
HEBREWS 4:15 KJV

For we do not have a high priest who is unable to empathize
with our weaknesses, but we have one who has been tempted
in every way, just as we are—yet he did not sin.
HEBREWS 4:15 NIV

It should greatly encourage you to know that Jesus stands before the Father, pleading your case: "Who is he who condemns? It is Christ who died, and furthermore is also risen, who is even at the right hand of God, who also makes intercession for us" (Romans 8:34 NKJV).

CONFIDENTLY ASKING FOR MERCY

When Jesus performed a great miracle in Peter's fishing boat, Peter knelt and said, "Depart from me, for I am a sinful man, O Lord!" (Luke 5:8 NKJV). Instead of despising him and departing, however, Jesus made him an outstanding follower. You may sometimes feel like Peter, like you have no right to be in the Lord's presence, let alone to request anything. But you "have boldness and confident access through faith in [Jesus]" (Ephesians 3:12 NASB).

Let us therefore come boldly unto the throne of grace,
that we may obtain mercy, and find grace to help in time of need.
HEBREWS 4:16 KJV

Let us then approach God's throne of grace with confidence,
so that we may receive mercy and find grace
to help us in our time of need.
HEBREWS 4:16 NIV

When Christians pray, they come before God's throne of grace—not His throne of judgment. You may be conscious of your failures and sins, but God urges you to come before Him confidently and without hesitation, expecting mercy and the power and grace to help you do better.

JESUS IS THE ONLY WAY

A major modern credo is that all faiths are equal, that all are wholly true paths to God. "Your faith may be true for you," you may hear, "but someone else's faith is their truth. To claim that yours is the only way is narrow-minded." But all faiths can't be true. Many are mutually exclusive: If they are true, then the others must be false. Christians should be aware that Jesus unequivocally declared that He alone is the way to God:

Jesus saith unto him, I am the way, the truth,
and the life: no man cometh unto the Father, but by me.
John 14:6 KJV

Jesus answered, "I am the way and the truth and the life.
No one comes to the Father except through me."
John 14:6 NIV

The Gospel of John says: "He who believes in the Son has everlasting life; and he who does not believe the Son shall not see life" (3:36 NKJV). If Jesus weren't the only way, there'd be no need to preach the gospel, as others would already be saved. But they aren't. This verse is therefore important to commit to memory.

SALVATION IN ONE NAME

According to many people, you can be saved by believing in Jesus, but you can also find salvation by following the teachings of Buddha. You can even walk in truth by worshipping an idol of mud. However, the apostles—whom Jesus personally sent out to preach—had an altogether different message. Peter boldly declared:

Neither is there salvation in any other:
for there is none other name under heaven
given among men, whereby we must be saved.
ACTS 4:12 KJV

"Salvation is found in no one else, for there is no other name under heaven given to mankind by which we must be saved."
ACTS 4:12 NIV

There is no name other than Jesus Christ, the *only* begotten Son of God, that can save a human soul from hell. As Paul explained, "For there is one God, and *one mediator* between God and men, the man Christ Jesus" (1 Timothy 2:5 KJV, emphasis added). Jesus stated, "All that ever came before me are thieves and robbers" (John 10:8 KJV), and said that after Him "shall arise false Christs, and false prophets" (Matthew 24:24 KJV).

CHRIST'S DIVINE QUALITIES

The passage below highlights Jesus' divine qualities. He isn't merely a mortal man but is the exact representation of the eternal, immortal God whom we can't see. By the power of His word, Jesus created the entire universe and will maintain it for endless ages.

Who is the image of the invisible God, the firstborn of every creature: for by him were all things created, that are in heaven, and that are in earth, visible and invisible, whether they be thrones, or dominions, or principalities, or powers: all things were created by him, and for him: and he is before all things, and by him all things consist.
COLOSSIANS 1:15–17 KJV

The Son is the image of the invisible God, the firstborn over all creation. For in him all things were created: things in heaven and on earth, visible and invisible, whether thrones or powers or rulers or authorities; all things have been created through him and for him. He is before all things, and in him all things hold together.
COLOSSIANS 1:15–17 NIV

You are to love and worship Jesus—and this passage lets you know why.

JESUS IS ETERNAL

God declared, "I am the LORD, I change not" (Malachi 3:6 KJV). The apostle James wrote that "he never changes or casts a shifting shadow" (James 1:17 NLT), and the psalmist said, "You are the same, and Your years will have no end" (Psalm 102:27 NKJV). God is eternal and perfect, utterly wonderful and unchanging. No person on earth is even remotely similar to Him. But Jesus Christ, exalted at the right hand of the Father, being of the same divine essence, is also eternally constant and unchanging.

Jesus Christ the same yesterday,
and to day, and for ever.
HEBREWS 13:8 KJV

Jesus Christ is the same yesterday and today and forever.
HEBREWS 13:8 NIV

This also means that Jesus remains forever glorious and able to exert His mighty power. He is still able to do miracles just as He did while on earth. You can always turn to Him for help: "He is able also to save them to the uttermost that come unto God by him, seeing he ever liveth to make intercession for them" (Hebrews 7:25 KJV).

POWER OF THE HOLY SPIRIT

Acts 1:8 (NIV) promises that "you will receive power when the Holy Spirit comes on you." While some modern believers sense sudden boldness when sharing the gospel, most don't. But note that Paul also said that "the love of God has been poured out within our hearts through the Holy Spirit who was given to us" (Romans 5:5 NASB), and he stated that "Christ's love compels us" (2 Corinthians 5:14 NIV).

But ye shall receive power, after that the Holy Ghost is come upon you: and ye shall be witnesses unto me both in Jerusalem, and in all Judaea, and in Samaria, and unto the uttermost part of the earth.
ACTS 1:8 KJV

"But you will receive power when the Holy Spirit comes on you; and you will be my witnesses in Jerusalem, and in all Judea and Samaria, and to the ends of the earth."
ACTS 1:8 NIV

There is tremendous power in the love of God. You may not feel a surge of boldness, but God does pour His great love into your heart, and that love should motivate you to share the good news with people.

WORSHIPPING ALMIGHTY GOD

Christians often become so busy, running around taking care of business, that they end up operating in their own strength. They lose sight of the fact that without God they can do nothing (John 15:5). Oftentimes, when the rush of the day seems ready to swallow you up, you need to pause, become quiet, and focus on the Lord.

Be still, and know that I am God: I will be exalted among the heathen, I will be exalted in the earth.
Psalm 46:10 KJV

"Be still, and know that I am God; I will be exalted among the nations, I will be exalted in the earth."
Psalm 46:10 NIV

It does you good to meditate on the Lord and know that He is God, that He is all-powerful, all-capable, and in charge of everything. His will shall be done on earth as it is in heaven (Matthew 6:10). "All the inhabitants of the earth are reputed as nothing; He does according to His will. . .among the inhabitants of the earth. No one can restrain His hand or say to Him, 'What have You done?'" (Daniel 4:35 NKJV).

GOD IS LOVE

The apostle John put it simply: "Whoever does not love does not know God" (1 John 4:8 NIV). Without love, you're nothing, no matter how much you accomplish. First Corinthians 13:2 (NASB) says, "If I have all faith, so as to remove mountains, but do not have love, I am nothing." Think of it. These are profound thoughts. Small wonder John stated that the most basic command for Christians is to believe and love: "This is His commandment, that we believe in the name of His Son Jesus Christ, and love one another" (1 John 3:23 NASB).

He that loveth not knoweth
not God; for God is love.
1 JOHN 4:8 KJV

Whoever does not love does
not know God, because God is love.
1 JOHN 4:8 NIV

Those three words, "God is love," are an endless mine of biblical insight. Whenever you wonder what God thinks about you, or if you worry that He's judging you, remember: "God is love." This is the most basic description of your heavenly Father, and it shapes all His views of you.

LOVE GOD WHOLEHEARTEDLY

According to Jesus, to love God is the most important commandment in the Bible (see Matthew 22:35–38). You are to love Him wholeheartedly. You are to be completely dedicated to God, seeking Him, fearing Him, and worshipping Him.

Hear, O Israel: The LORD our God is one LORD:
and thou shalt love the LORD thy God with all thine
heart, and with all thy soul, and with all thy might.
DEUTERONOMY 6:4–5 KJV

Hear, O Israel: The LORD our God, the LORD is one.
Love the LORD your God with all your heart and
with all your soul and with all your strength.
DEUTERONOMY 6:4–5 NIV

You don't need to try to work up this love on your own or tell yourself, "I must love God!" Rather, simply meditate on God and focus on His great love for you, His great mercy on you, and the wonderful things He's done for you. Then you'll find yourself loving Him. As the apostle John explained, "We love him, because he first loved us" (1 John 4:19 KJV).

LOVE OVERLOOKS FAULTS

When Peter asked Jesus if he should forgive someone for committing the same sin against him seven times, Jesus responded, "No, not seven times. . .but seventy times seven!" (Matthew 18:22 NLT). Years later, Peter explained that those who follow Jesus should love one another fervently because only such love is willing to forgive and overlook a multitude of sins (and some people do repeat the same sins many times).

And above all things have fervent charity among yourselves:
for charity shall cover the multitude of sins.
1 PETER 4:8 KJV

Above all, love each other deeply, because love
covers over a multitude of sins.
1 PETER 4:8 NIV

Love "keeps no record of being wronged" (1 Corinthians 13:5 NLT). You could be wronged seventy-seven times in one day, but when you refuse to keep a tally of another person's sins, you demonstrate the kind of love Jesus desires you to have. If you love greatly and forgive freely, others will trust you and relax around you. As a result, they will be more likely to forgive your mistakes and sins as well.

LOVE YOUR FELLOW MAN

This command, tucked away in an obscure corner of Leviticus, was a prime candidate for being overlooked. But tireless Jewish scribes, seeking treasures in the Word of God, realized that the words "Thou shalt love thy neighbour as thyself" were at the very heart of God's Law. Jesus would later say that it was the greatest of all commandments, second only to loving God (Matthew 22:36–40).

Thou shalt not avenge, nor bear any grudge against the children of thy people, but thou shalt love thy neighbour as thyself.
Leviticus 19:18 KJV

"Do not seek revenge or bear a grudge against anyone among your people, but love your neighbor as yourself."
Leviticus 19:18 NIV

The first half of the verse explains how far love is to go. Not only are you *not* to actively seek and wreak revenge on your fellow man, you are not even to nurse a grudge against him in your heart. Instead, you are to love your neighbor as you love yourself—which means constantly looking out for them, doing things to help them, and doing no harm to them.

LAYING DOWN YOUR LIFE

To "lay down your life" means to die to yourself—to avoid only seeking your own comforts, wants, and goals. Instead of grasping at whatever you can to save your life, you unhook your fingers from those things and set them on the ground—just like Jesus voluntarily laid Himself on the cross and took the nails in His hands and feet. It takes the love of God to motivate you to do this.

Hereby perceive we the love of God, because he laid down his life for us: and we ought to lay down our lives for the brethren.
1 JOHN 3:16 KJV

This is how we know what love is: Jesus Christ laid down his life for us. And we ought to lay down our lives for our brothers and sisters.
1 JOHN 3:16 NIV

You can "lay down your life" in many small ways, not just in one heroic act such as throwing yourself in front of a truck to prevent someone else from being killed. You "lay down your life" every time you set aside your rights and desires and put others ahead of yourself.

LOVE YOUR ENEMIES

Jesus said, "Love your enemies, do good to them which hate you, bless them that curse you, and pray for them which despitefully use you" (Luke 6:27–28 KJV). But even many Christians think this is too idealistic. They believe that Jesus only had such love because He was perfect, and they don't believe He actually expects ordinary people to love their enemies. But Jesus set an example for you to follow, and He repeated His command later in Luke 6:

> *But love ye your enemies, and do good, and lend, hoping for nothing again; and your reward shall be great, and ye shall be the children of the Highest: for he is kind unto the unthankful and to the evil.*
>
> LUKE 6:35 KJV

> *"But love your enemies, do good to them, and lend to them without expecting to get anything back. Then your reward will be great, and you will be children of the Most High, because he is kind to the ungrateful and wicked."*
>
> LUKE 6:35 NIV

If you truly want to follow Jesus and live like God's child, then you will follow His command and example and love like He loves—even the thankless and the disobedient.

DOING UNTO OTHERS

People often think nothing of doing selfish or mean things to others. But when others do those same things to them, they indignantly protest. Think for a moment of a comment someone made to you that really stung. Now that you have it firmly fixed in your mind, recall times that you did something similar to others. By saying the following, Jesus was stressing the value of putting yourself in someone else's shoes:

Therefore all things whatsoever ye would that
men should do to you, do ye even so to them:
for this is the law and the prophets.
MATTHEW 7:12 KJV

"So in everything, do to others what you would have them
do to you, for this sums up the Law and the Prophets."
MATTHEW 7:12 NIV

If you do as Jesus instructed in this verse, you've grasped the whole purpose of the books of the Law and all the writings of the prophets. Solomon added, "Also do not take to heart everything people say, lest you hear your servant cursing you. For many times, also, your own heart has known that even you have cursed others" (Ecclesiastes 7:21–22 NKJV).

THE WORD IN YOUR HEART

Believers so frequently quote this verse in reference to memorizing Bible passages that "hiding the Word in their heart" has become synonymous with memorizing the Word. But this verse means more than simply scripture memorization. It implies absorbing God's instructions into the core of your being—allowing His Spirit to write them on your heart—with the clear intent to remember and obey them.

Thy word have I hid in mine heart,
that I might not sin against thee.
PSALM 119:11 KJV

I have hidden your word in my heart
that I might not sin against you.
PSALM 119:11 NIV

Memorizing God's Word gives the Holy Spirit something to remind you of. When you have to make an ethical or moral decision, it can be hard to know what to do if you have no idea what God says about it. But once you're aware of His will, the Holy Spirit can bring it to your mind when you need it: "The Holy Spirit, whom the Father will send in My name, He will teach you all things, and bring to your remembrance all that I said to you" (John 14:26 NASB).

EYES TO BEHOLD

Many people read the Bible with blinders on. Paul wrote that "a veil lies over their heart; but whenever a person turns to the Lord, the veil is taken away" (2 Corinthians 3:15–16 NASB). If you're tired or distracted or in a hurry, you can read an entire chapter and not grasp a thing it said—or even remember what it said. It helps immensely to have the Spirit of Christ in your heart, illuminating your mind and enabling you to grasp His Word. But even believers need to pray for the Lord to help them understand Bible passages. The writer of Psalm 119 did just that:

Open thou mine eyes, that I may behold
wondrous things out of thy law.
PSALM 119:18 KJV

Open my eyes that I may see wonderful things in your law.
PSALM 119:18 NIV

So pray and ask God to reveal truth in His Word to you. Two disciples on the road to Emmaus had revelations when Jesus was explaining the meaning of key passages: "And He opened their understanding, that they might comprehend the Scriptures" (Luke 24:45 NKJV). Ask the Lord to open your eyes and your understanding today.

LIGHT FOR YOUR PATH

Life can be very difficult at times, and the way uncertain. With so many options to choose from and no obvious clues as to what outcome they lead to, it can be hard to know which way to go. It's like walking in darkness. Jesus said, "During the day people can walk safely. They can see because they have the light of this world. But at night there is danger of stumbling because they have no light" (John 11:9–10 NLT). That's why it helps to have God's Word lighting the way.

Thy word is a lamp unto my feet,
and a light unto my path.
PSALM 119:105 KJV

Your word is a lamp for my feet,
a light on my path.
PSALM 119:105 NIV

This verse says that God's Word is "a light on [your] path." A few verses later, the psalmist explains: "The unfolding of Your words gives light; it gives understanding to the simple" (Psalm 119:130 NASB). The "light" referred to here is the ability to understand difficult problems in light of God's Word and to know what you should choose.

FOOD FOR YOUR SPIRIT

The Bible teaches that the Word of God gives energy to your spirit: "Man shall not live by bread alone; but man lives by every word that proceeds from the mouth of the LORD" (Deuteronomy 8:3 NKJV). An unknown psalmist wrote, "How sweet are Your words to my taste, sweeter than honey to my mouth!" (Psalm 119:103 NKJV). And after God told Ezekiel to "fill your stomach with this scroll that I give you," Ezekiel said, "I ate, and it was in my mouth like honey in sweetness" (Ezekiel 3:3 NKJV).

Thy words were found, and I did eat them; and thy word was unto me the joy and rejoicing of mine heart: for I am called by thy name, O LORD God of hosts.
JEREMIAH 15:16 KJV

When your words came, I ate them; they were my joy and my heart's delight, for I bear your name, LORD God Almighty.
JEREMIAH 15:16 NIV

Just as you hunger for food several times a day, you are to constantly hunger for spiritual nourishment. You wouldn't expect to get by with one short meal a week, would you?

PACKED WITH POWER

In his book *Mere Christianity*, C. S. Lewis said that we must dispense with pious statements such as saying that Jesus was merely "a great moral teacher." He stated that a man who said the sorts of things Jesus said was either a madman, a devil from hell, or else He was exactly who He claimed to be—Lord and God. Jesus said He was humble (Matthew 11:29), yet He claimed that "the words that I speak unto you, they are spirit, and they are life" (John 6:63 KJV). These aren't humble claims. . .unless they're true.

It is the spirit that quickeneth;
the flesh profiteth nothing: the words that I
speak unto you, they are spirit, and they are life.
JOHN 6:63 KJV

"The Spirit gives life; the flesh counts for nothing. The words
I have spoken to you—they are full of the Spirit and life."
JOHN 6:63 NIV

Some people complained to Jesus, "You say, 'Anyone who obeys my teaching will never die!' . . . Who do you think you are?" (John 8:52–53 NLT). Jesus made a claim to being divine. Hence His words give eternal life to those who believe and obey them.

POSSESSED BY GOD

Many people wonder if the prophets were aware they were speaking the very words of God. The answer is yes, they were. They had to be to say, "Thus saith the LORD. . ." It must have been overwhelming to realize that God was speaking scripture through them. King David declared:

The Spirit of the LORD spake by me,
and his word was in my tongue.
2 SAMUEL 23:2 KJV

"The Spirit of the LORD spoke through me;
his word was on my tongue."
2 SAMUEL 23:2 NIV

Elsewhere, a psalmist said, "My tongue is the pen of a ready writer" (Psalm 45:1 KJV). It was as if his mouth was an instrument in the hand of God, and it simply poured forth His words. The Spirit of God flowed through David's tongue, like ink through a pen. He and other inspired men were very aware of the presence of God in their lives, and they knew God trusted them with something truly powerful and holy.

SCRIPTURE IS INSPIRED BY GOD

Jesus said, "Assuredly, I say to you, till heaven and earth pass away, one jot or one tittle will by no means pass from the law till all is fulfilled" (Matthew 5:18 NKJV). The Old Testament was written in Hebrew text, and a "jot" meant the letter *yod* (Psalm 119:73), which was as small as an apostrophe and equivalent to *iota*, the smallest letter in the Greek alphabet. A "tittle" was a decorative horn on Hebrew letters. So Jesus was saying that every bit of the holy writings, down to the most insignificant stroke of ink, was inspired. The Bible contains no false statements.

All scripture is given by inspiration of God,
and is profitable for doctrine, for reproof,
for correction, for instruction in righteousness.
2 Timothy 3:16 KJV

All Scripture is God-breathed and is useful for teaching,
rebuking, correcting and training in righteousness.
2 Timothy 3:16 NIV

Small wonder that the scriptures are considered such an authority in all matters pertaining to life and godliness, and that they are useful for teaching disciples, rebuking heretics, correcting the misguided, and training sincere followers in righteousness.

INSPIRATION AND PERSONALITY

You might wonder how much God inspired the books of the Bible—and how much they reflect the personalities of the men God used to record them. For example, Jeremiah's scroll is a mishmash, largely out of order, whereas Ezekiel's scroll is meticulously dated and organized; Luke was a physician, and his Gospel contains abundant medical terms; Mark's Gospel reflects Peter's personality; and John's Greek grammar in Revelation is so bad it's barbaric. But Peter wrote:

For the prophecy came not in old time by the will of man:
but holy men of God spake as they were moved by the Holy Ghost.
2 PETER 1:21 KJV

For prophecy never had its origin in the human will,
but prophets, though human, spoke from God as
they were carried along by the Holy Spirit.
2 PETER 1:21 NIV

While the Bible books all bear the imprint of their writers' personalities, the Bible is still wholly inspired. God designed the writers' DNA and personalities, after all. It's clear that He incorporated the cultural backgrounds, character traits, and mannerisms of the men and women He chose to use into the message He delivered through them.

RECEIVING REVELATIONS

Earlier, we discussed the verse, "Open my eyes that I may see wonderful things in your law" (Psalm 119:18 NIV). It pertained to receiving life-giving, encouraging insights from the Word of God, the Bible. The verse below, on the other hand, addresses your receiving revelations—of "great and unsearchable things"—directly from your heavenly Father. He says in Jeremiah:

Call unto me, and I will answer thee, and show thee great and mighty things, which thou knowest not.
JEREMIAH 33:3 KJV

"Call to me and I will answer you and tell you great and unsearchable things you do not know."
JEREMIAH 33:3 NIV

You don't have to be hyperspiritual to desire insights from the Holy Spirit or to have God impress a message on your heart. After all, Paul prayed for *all* Christians "that the God of our Lord Jesus Christ. . .may give to you the spirit of wisdom and *revelation* in the knowledge of Him, the eyes of your *understanding* being *enlightened*; that you may know. . .the riches of the glory of His inheritance" (Ephesians 1:17–18 NKJV, emphasis added).

SEEKING THE LORD

The verse below states, "Seek the Lord *and* his strength." Many people only cry out to God to manifest His power in their lives. While it's good that they acknowledge their need, such a prayer primarily seeks to *use* God. People want to tap into His power, like the woman who crept up behind Jesus and touched His garment. She wanted healing, but she also wanted to avoid a personal encounter (Matthew 9:20–22). But the Bible teaches that you are first to "seek the Lord" then seek His strength.

Seek the Lord and his strength,
seek his face continually.
1 Chronicles 16:11 KJV

Look to the Lord and his strength;
seek his face always.
1 Chronicles 16:11 NIV

Note also that the verse says to "seek his face continually." Praying to God isn't something you should do just in isolated moments in the morning or evening. You should seek to be in the presence of the Lord all day long. This is what the verse "Pray without ceasing" (1 Thessalonians 5:17 KJV) means. You don't have to be constantly speaking words, but you should be constantly aware of the Lord and be open to His Spirit.

CLAIMING A MIRACLE

The verse below is a powerful promise, but it also confuses many believers. Because it says, "believe that you have received it," many Christians assume that they are to proclaim that their prayer has been answered—for healing or some other miracle—before they have any evidence they've received it. They think if they keep repeating "I'm healed!" long enough, refusing to doubt, the miracle will eventually materialize. This works for some people but not for most.

Therefore I say unto you, What things soever ye desire, when ye pray, believe that ye receive them, and ye shall have them.
MARK 11:24 KJV

"Therefore I tell you, whatever you ask for in prayer, believe that you have received it, and it will be yours."
MARK 11:24 NIV

Jesus told two blind men who wanted to see, "According to your faith be it unto you" (Matthew 9:29 KJV), so it's clear that the person claiming a miracle must actually believe God has granted it, not merely be repeating the claim in an effort to hypnotize themselves or to work up faith they don't have. Ask God to increase your faith (see Luke 17:5).

WHATEVER YOU ASK

God is forgiving and compassionate, but if you want Him to answer your prayers, you must repent of any sin and be in right relation with Him. A blind man Jesus had healed said, "God doesn't listen to sinners, but he is ready to hear those who worship him and do his will" (John 9:31 NLT). You must be obedient to God. The following passage brings this out clearly:

Beloved, if our heart condemn us not, then have we confidence toward God. And whatsoever we ask, we receive of him, because we keep his commandments, and do those things that are pleasing in his sight.
1 JOHN 3:21–22 KJV

Dear friends, if our hearts do not condemn us, we have confidence before God and receive from him anything we ask, because we keep his commands and do what pleases him.
1 JOHN 3:21–22 NIV

If you've been asking God for something and have repented of any sin you're aware of, then you can have confidence that He will grant "anything [you] ask." Of course, what you're praying for must also be within His will.

PRAYING WITHIN GOD'S WILL

If it's God's will for you to have what you're requesting, He will give it to you. If you're certain He hears your prayer—hears it with the intent to answer—He definitely will answer it. The apostle John taught this when he wrote:

And this is the confidence that we have in him, that,
if we ask any thing according to his will, he heareth us:
and if we know that he hear us, whatsoever we ask,
we know that we have the petitions that we desired of him.
1 John 5:14–15 KJV

This is the confidence we have in approaching God:
that if we ask anything according to his will, he hears us.
And if we know that he hears us—whatever we ask—
we know that we have what we asked of him.
1 John 5:14–15 NIV

Psalm 37:4 (KJV) says, "Delight thyself also in the Lord: and he shall give thee the desires of thine heart." Many Christians lust for things and claim that God has vowed to give them all their desires. But don't forget that you are first to delight yourself in the Lord—which means choosing His will. If you do this, you won't desire selfish things to begin with.

AGREEING IN PRAYER

There's power in united prayer. Jesus promised that if believers agree about something in prayer, God will grant their petition. But remember, this isn't a stand-alone promise. God isn't merely doing a head count. Those uniting themselves in prayer must have faith when they pray, be obedient to God, and be requesting something within His will.

Again I say unto you, That if two of you shall agree on earth as touching any thing that they shall ask, it shall be done for them of my Father which is in heaven. For where two or three are gathered together in my name, there am I in the midst of them.
MATTHEW 18:19–20 KJV

"Again, truly I tell you that if two of you on earth agree about anything they ask for, it will be done for them by my Father in heaven. For where two or three gather in my name, there am I with them."
MATTHEW 18:19–20 NIV

Why should you ask others to join with you in prayer if God can answer your prayers alone? Because there's strength in unity (see Ecclesiastes 4:12).

ANSWERING BEFORE YOU PRAY

Jesus said, "When you pray, don't babble on and on. . .for your Father knows exactly what you need even before you ask him!" (Matthew 6:7–8 NLT). So new Christians often ask, "Why should I pray at all if God already knows what I need?" The answer is that it does you much good to be concerned about your problems, to look to God for help, and to verbalize your needs. But because God already knows what you need, He can answer your prayers before you even begin.

And it shall come to pass, that before they call,
I will answer; and while they are yet speaking, I will hear.
ISAIAH 65:24 KJV

"Before they call I will answer;
while they are still speaking I will hear."
ISAIAH 65:24 NIV

Don't ever put off prayer. God frequently allows you to encounter difficulties to test you, to see if you will stir yourself up to call out to Him. Isaiah described a low point in Israel's history, saying, "There is no one who calls on Your name, who stirs himself to take hold of You" (Isaiah 64:7 NASB). Don't be like the people of Israel in Isaiah's day.

SEEKING GOD WHOLEHEARTEDLY

Isaiah observed, "Truly You are God, who hide Yourself" (Isaiah 45:15 NKJV). Because of His people's sin or negligence, God often withdraws beyond their ability to perceive Him, which then forces them to search for Him. Paul said that people "should seek the Lord, in the hope that they might. . .find Him, though He is not far from each one of us" (Acts 17:27 NKJV). God draws very close to those seeking Him.

And ye shall seek me, and find me,
when ye shall search for me with all your heart.
JEREMIAH 29:13 KJV

"You will seek me and find me when
you seek me with all your heart."
JEREMIAH 29:13 NIV

So often, however, people seek God only for a brief time. They don't actually keep at it until they find Him. But the Lord explains that His children need to persist in searching for Him. When you search for God with all your heart, don't give up if you don't succeed immediately. Keep at it. Keep seeking the Lord until you know you've touched Him.

ASK, AND IT SHALL BE GIVEN

In the NIV passage below, Jesus said, "Ask and it will be given to you" (Matthew 7:7). However, the New Living Translation captures the meaning of the Greek words better, saying, "*Keep on asking*, and you will receive what you ask for" (emphasis added).

Ask, and it shall be given you; seek, and ye shall find; knock, and it shall be opened unto you: for every one that asketh receiveth; and he that seeketh findeth; and to him that knocketh it shall be opened.
MATTHEW 7:7–8 KJV

"Ask and it will be given to you; seek and you will find; knock and the door will be opened to you. For everyone who asks receives; the one who seeks finds; and to the one who knocks, the door will be opened."
MATTHEW 7:7–8 NIV

Jesus didn't promise that you'd always get an answer to prayer instantly. You often have to be very persistent. As for His saying, "to the one who knocks, the door will be opened," read His parable about a persistent man knocking on a friend's door at midnight, asking for three loaves of bread (see Luke 11:5–8).

THE LORD'S PRAYER

There's a slightly different version of the Lord's Prayer in Luke 11:1–4, but the one recorded in Matthew is the best known. It covers all the bases—praising God, yielding to His will, praying for your needs, asking for forgiveness, and requesting deliverance from evil.

Our Father which art in heaven, Hallowed be thy name. Thy kingdom come, thy will be done in earth, as it is in heaven. Give us this day our daily bread. And forgive us our debts, as we forgive our debtors. And lead us not into temptation, but deliver us from evil: For thine is the kingdom, and the power, and the glory, for ever. Amen.
MATTHEW 6:9–13 KJV

"Our Father in heaven, hallowed be your name, your kingdom come, your will be done, on earth as it is in heaven. Give us today our daily bread. And forgive us our debts, as we also have forgiven our debtors. And lead us not into temptation, but deliver us from the evil one."
MATTHEW 6:9–13 NIV

Jesus gave this as a model of how to pray, but it's not meant to be simply quoted like some magical mantra. Meditate on the meaning of the words as you quote them.

PERILS OF PRAYERLESSNESS

When you fail to pray, you miss God's guidance and warnings. When the Gibeonites came to trick the Israelites into making a peace treaty, they "did not ask counsel of the Lord. So Joshua . . .made a covenant with them" (Joshua 9:14–15 NKJV). This could have been avoided had they only prayed. Samuel told the Israelites, "Far be it from me that I should sin against the Lord in ceasing to pray for you" (1 Samuel 12:23 NKJV). The following verse describes King Rehoboam:

And he did evil, because he prepared
not his heart to seek the Lord.
2 Chronicles 12:14 KJV

He did evil because he had not set
his heart on seeking the Lord.
2 Chronicles 12:14 NIV

Ignoring God and rushing into your day without prayer may start as isolated incidents, but eventually it becomes an ingrained habit—and it always precedes spiritual decline. Rehoboam didn't set his heart on seeking God, and as a result he "forsook the law of the Lord, and all Israel along with him" (2 Chronicles 12:1 NKJV).

WISDOM AND DECISION-MAKING

One night King Solomon had a dream in which God said to him, "What do you want? Ask, and I will give it to you!" (1 Kings 3:5 NLT). Solomon asked God for wisdom so he could rule Israel prudently, so God gave it. And the good news is He's still willing to give wisdom to anyone who asks.

If any of you lack wisdom, let him ask of God, that giveth to all men liberally, and upbraideth not; and it shall be given him.
JAMES 1:5 KJV

If any of you lacks wisdom, you should ask God, who gives generously to all without finding fault, and it will be given to you.
JAMES 1:5 NIV

God can give you "the word of wisdom" (1 Corinthians 12:8 KJV). He can give you piercing insights into profound mysteries, and He can also make you wiser overall. But for the latter, God requires your cooperation: You must diligently study. To Daniel and his three friends, "God gave these four young men an unusual aptitude for understanding every aspect of literature and wisdom" (Daniel 1:17 NLT). But they had also to study "for three years" (verse 5).

EXPECTING WITHOUT VACILLATING

Jesus said that whoever prays "and does not doubt in his heart. . . will have whatever he says" (Mark 11:23 NKJV). On the other hand, the Bible teaches that if you doubt, rather than receiving whatever you pray for, you'll receive nothing. Faith is absolutely essential. James cautioned:

But let him ask in faith, nothing wavering. For he that wavereth is like a wave of the sea driven with the wind and tossed. For let not that man think that he shall receive any thing of the Lord. A double minded man is unstable in all his ways.
JAMES 1:6–8 KJV

But when you ask, you must believe and not doubt, because the one who doubts is like a wave of the sea, blown and tossed by the wind. That person should not expect to receive anything from the Lord. Such a person is double-minded and unstable in all they do.
JAMES 1:6–8 NIV

You may say, "But I often doubt, so I'll never get anything. Why didn't God give me greater faith?" However, the issue isn't that you're assaulted by doubts—all believers are—but whether or not you hold up the "shield of faith" (Ephesians 6:16) to prevent those doubts from lodging in your mind.

ENTRUSTING PLANS TO GOD

What does "committing your way to the Lord" mean? Many Christians use this phrase but don't understand what it's really saying. To "commit" something to someone is to hand it over to that person for his safekeeping, to entrust it to him, to place it under his management or protection. When you "commit your way to the Lord," you're surrendering your plans and actions to God.

Commit thy way unto the Lord;
trust also in him; and he shall bring it to pass.
Psalm 37:5 KJV

Commit your way to the Lord; trust in him and he will do this.
Psalm 37:5 NIV

If you're willing to release your tight grip on your desires, refrain from controlling them, and allow God to do what He desires with them, He's not only able to establish your plans and make sure they happen, but He can also bring about the best possible results. But be advised: by committing your ways to God you're saying, "Your will be done" (Matthew 26:42 NKJV), so if your plans aren't His will, committing them to Him lets Him change them or dispose of them.

FLYING BLIND

The verse below may be easy to memorize, but it can be difficult to live. When you trust God with all your heart and don't put any confidence in your own understanding, you'll sometimes find yourself in situations where you're like a pilot flying blind through thick clouds between jagged mountains, trusting in your instruments. This takes great faith, and you have to resist the urge to panic.

Trust in the LORD with all thine heart; and lean not unto thine own understanding. In all thy ways acknowledge him, and he shall direct thy paths.
PROVERBS 3:5–6 KJV

Trust in the LORD with all your heart and lean not on your own understanding; in all your ways submit to him, and he will make your paths straight.
PROVERBS 3:5–6 NIV

There is a promise included in this verse. If you continuously submit to the Lord and acknowledge His sovereignty, He will give you clear directions, even if you're flying blind. He says, "I will bring the blind by a way they did not know; I will lead them in paths they have not known. I will make darkness light before them" (Isaiah 42:16 NKJV).

GOD IS YOUR RULER

For several hundred years, God used judges to rule Israel. Then the Israelites demanded that the prophet Samuel give them a king, like other nations. They also wanted a standing army to defend themselves. This grieved Samuel, but God told him, "Do everything they say to you. . .for they are rejecting me, not you. They don't want me to be their king any longer" (1 Samuel 8:7 NLT). Earlier, they had asked Gideon to be their king:

And Gideon said unto them, I will not
rule over you, neither shall my son rule
over you: the LORD shall rule over you.
JUDGES 8:23 KJV

But Gideon told them, "I will not rule
over you, nor will my son rule over you.
The LORD will rule over you."
JUDGES 8:23 NIV

God wanted to rule over His people, but they didn't like that because it meant trusting Him to do miracles to defend them. You will face similar tests. Often you'll want to trust natural means for protection. But God desires to lead you by His Spirit and to be your protector.

GOD'S WAYS VERSUS MAN'S WAYS

Many Christians pray primarily to ask the Lord to bless their plans, but God won't always do that. He cautions that His ways are not man's ways. Man's ways are self-centered and in line with the world's goals and methods, but God's ways are loving and selfless.

For my thoughts are not your thoughts, neither are your ways my ways, saith the LORD. For as the heavens are higher than the earth, so are my ways higher than your ways, and my thoughts than your thoughts.
ISAIAH 55:8–9 KJV

"For my thoughts are not your thoughts, neither are your ways my ways," declares the LORD. "As the heavens are higher than the earth, so are my ways higher than your ways and my thoughts than your thoughts."
ISAIAH 55:8–9 NIV

God requires you "to love the LORD your God, to walk in all His ways, and to hold fast to Him" (Deuteronomy 11:22 NKJV). As His son, you are to walk in His ways, "to walk in the same manner as He walked" (1 John 2:6 NASB).

JUDGING PEOPLE'S FRUIT

Jesus explained that even though wolves (religious con men) might come disguised as sheep, over time you can still tell the difference between them and true Christians by the fruit they bear. Even if a thornbush was disguised as a grape vine, it would never bear grapes. Jesus said, "A good tree produces good fruit, and a bad tree produces bad fruit" (Matthew 7:17 NLT). He summed it up, saying, "Just as you can identify a tree by its fruit, so you can identify people by their actions" (verse 20 NLT). Or, as the KJV and NIV put it:

Wherefore by their fruits ye shall know them.
MATTHEW 7:20 KJV

"Thus, by their fruit you will recognize them."
MATTHEW 7:20 NIV

It takes time to see where some people are at in their relationship with the Lord. Jesus explained this principle in the parable of the wheat and the tares in Matthew 13:24–30. When still growing, tares (a plant called darnel) look so much like wheat that it's difficult to tell the difference. But when they're ready for harvest, the difference is clear.

LOOKING AT THE HEART

God had informed Samuel that He would choose a new king for Israel, so Samuel went to Bethlehem and met Jesse and his sons. When Samuel saw Jesse's oldest son, Eliab—tall, strong, and handsome—he immediately concluded that Eliab was the chosen one. But God told him:

Look not on his countenance, or on the height of his stature; because I have refused him: for the LORD seeth not as man seeth; for man looketh on the outward appearance, but the LORD looketh on the heart.
1 SAMUEL 16:7 KJV

"Do not consider his appearance or his height, for I have rejected him. The LORD does not look at the things people look at. People look at the outward appearance, but the LORD looks at the heart."
1 SAMUEL 16:7 NIV

Often, even believers look on outward appearances. But in James 2:1–4, Christians are warned not to give better treatment to a rich man in expensive robes than to a poor man in ragged clothing. Likewise, Peter advised Christian women not to try to impress others by outward beauty, but to let their inner beauty shine forth (see 1 Peter 3:3–4).

RIGHTEOUS JUDGMENT

Many Christians base their entire theology of discernment and judging on one verse—Matthew 7:1—in fact, on just these two words: "judge not." But clearly believers are called to judge certain matters and situations. Paul says in 1 Corinthians 10:15 (KJV), "Judge ye what I say." (See also 1 Corinthians 5:9–13 and 6:1–5, where Paul says that even the least esteemed in the church are qualified to judge matters.)

Judge not, that ye be not judged. For with what judgment ye judge, ye shall be judged: and with what measure ye mete, it shall be measured to you again.
MATTHEW 7:1–2 KJV

"Do not judge, or you too will be judged. For in the same way you judge others, you will be judged, and with the measure you use, it will be measured to you."
MATTHEW 7:1–2 NIV

Nevertheless, knowing that you will be judged in the same way you judge others ought to cause you to be merciful, just, and fair to others. Believers are to judge using love and wisdom—and to depend on God's wisdom. Jesus said, "Judge not according to the appearance, but judge righteous judgment" (John 7:24 KJV).

A TIME FOR EVERYTHING

As this famous passage in Ecclesiastes says, there is a time for everything: "A time to plant, and a time to pluck what is planted... a time to break down, and a time to build up; a time to weep, and a time to laugh" (Ecclesiastes 3:2–4 NKJV).

To every thing there is a season, and a time
to every purpose under the heaven.
ECCLESIASTES 3:1 KJV

There is a time for everything, and a season
for every activity under the heavens.
ECCLESIASTES 3:1 NIV

How do you know when it's time to do something, or when it isn't the right time to do it? Solomon stated, "A wise man's heart discerns both time and judgment" (Ecclesiastes 8:5 NKJV). You must judge from the circumstances what's appropriate. You must also listen to God, who may speak to you in "a still small voice" (1 Kings 19:12 KJV) or give you the distinct impression, "This is the way, walk in it" (Isaiah 30:21 NASB).

BLESSING FOR TRUSTING GOD

Naomi and her husband and two sons had been living in Moab, but after all the men died, she returned to Israel. One of her Moabite daughters-in-law, Ruth, returned with her. Ruth abandoned her country and her gods to look after Naomi. It was barley harvest, so once they were back in Naomi's village, Ruth went out gleaning stalks of barley for food. Boaz, the owner of the field, praised her, saying:

The LORD recompense thy work, and a full
reward be given thee of the LORD God of Israel,
under whose wings thou art come to trust.
RUTH 2:12 KJV

"May the LORD repay you for what you have done.
May you be richly rewarded by the LORD, the God of Israel,
under whose wings you have come to take refuge."
RUTH 2:12 NIV

This blessing holds true for all those who have come to trust in God, all who "[dwell] in the shelter of the Most High" (Psalm 91:1 NASB). The Bible promises, "He will cover you with His pinions, and under His wings you may seek refuge" (Psalm 91:4 NASB; see also Psalm 36:7).

GOD'S GOOD THOUGHTS

Often when you're going through a difficult time, you think that God has it in for you, that He is judging you for some sin. And though you repeatedly repent, there seems to be no way to get Him to favor and bless you. But this whole attitude is wrong. God *loves* you, and if you have Christ in your heart and are sincerely trying to follow Him, God's heart is set on blessing you. Take comfort in the following promise:

For I know the thoughts that I think toward you,
saith the LORD, thoughts of peace, and not of
evil, to give you an expected end.
JEREMIAH 29:11 KJV

"For I know the plans I have for you," declares the LORD,
"plans to prosper you and not to harm you,
plans to give you hope and a future."
JEREMIAH 29:11 NIV

Why then do you have constant problems, suffer lack, or feel like God is judging you? Often God is simply disciplining you (see Hebrews 12:4–11). But even that is proof that you're His child and that He loves you!

GOD'S HAND ON YOUR LIFE

The verse below promises that when you faithfully look to God, His hand will be on your life, protecting you, providing for you, and leading you. You may still occasionally go through lean times because God is testing you and chastising you as a beloved child, but His love will never depart from you. He will always watch over you, constantly blessing you in a multitude of ways.

The hand of our God is upon all them for good that seek him; but his power and his wrath is against all them that forsake him.
Ezra 8:22 KJV

"The gracious hand of our God is on everyone who looks to him, but his great anger is against all who forsake him."
Ezra 8:22 NIV

However, if you turn away from the Lord, blatantly disobey Him, and consistently neglect to seek Him in prayer, He will discipline you to bring you back. Even when He feels anger, however, your heavenly Father is motivated by mercy. Habakkuk prayed, "O Lord. . .in wrath remember mercy" (Habakkuk 3:2 NKJV), and you can be certain that He does.

FOCUSING ON GOD

Christians very often quote the verse here during times of severe testing. It's a powerful promise that many have clung to when trouble was all around: If you will keep your mind focused on God and trust steadfastly in Him, He will give you a completely tranquil mind even though storms are raging near you.

Thou wilt keep him in perfect peace, whose mind
is stayed on thee: because he trusteth in thee.
ISAIAH 26:3 KJV

You will keep in perfect peace those whose minds
are steadfast, because they trust in you.
ISAIAH 26:3 NIV

If you'll take the time to commit this verse to memory, you'll gain a valuable counselor that will bring you much peace during troubled times. The NIV would have been a little clearer had it said, "steadfastly focused on you," instead of simply "steadfast"—but the thought is essentially there.

PEACE IN THE STORM

When you're going through troubled times, your emotions are often turbulent and it's difficult to have a rational view of issues. This is precisely the time that you need the peace of God to calm your mind. And when it does, you won't know how you suddenly have peace, because you still don't know how your problems will be resolved—but in that moment great tranquility descends upon you, and you're calm even though the storm continues raging.

And the peace of God, which passeth all understanding, shall keep your hearts and minds through Christ Jesus.
PHILIPPIANS 4:7 KJV

And the peace of God, which transcends all understanding, will guard your hearts and your minds in Christ Jesus.
PHILIPPIANS 4:7 NIV

What does the Bible mean when it says that God's peace will guard your heart and your mind? Your "mind" refers to your conscious thoughts over which you have a large measure of control, and your "heart" refers to your deep, subconscious mind, which often seems to be beyond your control but which reflects the attitudes and habits you have nurtured over many years. God is able to guard both with His peace.

LOVING HEART, SOUND MIND

This verse can be a great comfort when you're under terrific mental pressure, when you're attacked by waves of fear, or when you feel like you're on the verge of losing your sanity. It reassures you that your fears aren't from God but are attacks of the enemy—and are to be rejected and refused. You know from Acts 1:8 that the Holy Spirit gives you power. And it's wonderful to have the authority to claim that a sound mind is your right, something you can insist on as you walk in Christ.

For God hath not given us the spirit of fear;
but of power, and of love, and of a sound mind.
2 TIMOTHY 1:7 KJV

For the Spirit God gave us does not make us timid,
but gives us power, love and self-discipline.
2 TIMOTHY 1:7 NIV

The NIV has "self-discipline" instead of "sound mind." So which is most accurate? Well, the NASB—which even Bible skeptics accept as a very accurate translation—has the word *discipline* here but has a translation note that adds, "Or sound judgment." So both meanings are likely accurate.

HAVING GREAT PEACE

So far, you've learned that you can have great peace by focusing your mind on God and also by walking in Christ and praying for Him to give you peace. But there's another clue on how you can obtain God's peace: by loving His Word. This verse asserts that those who love the scriptures and meditate on them will have great peace, and nothing shall cause them to fall:

Great peace have they which love thy law:
and nothing shall offend them.
Psalm 119:165 KJV

Great peace have those who love your law,
and nothing can make them stumble.
Psalm 119:165 NIV

The KJV says, "nothing shall offend them," but the Hebrew words used here literally mean "they have no stumbling block." In other words, if you keep your mind and heart filled with the Word of God, the enemy of your soul won't be able to trip you up and make you fall. You'll walk with great peace, confidence, and self-control, and the devil won't be able to get a rock under your feet to twist your ankle and bring you down.

GIVING GOD YOUR CARES

This brief scripture is greatly beloved, as it contains a very powerful message. In it, Peter acknowledges that believers will frequently be beset by cares, worries, and anxieties, but he advises you to cast your troubled thoughts upon the Lord. You can do this, trusting that God will look after all your problems and work them out because of one simple fact: God cares for you.

Casting all your care upon him;
for he careth for you.
1 PETER 5:7 KJV

Cast all your anxiety on him
because he cares for you.
1 PETER 5:7 NIV

David declares, "The LORD is thy keeper," and he informs you, "Behold, he that keepeth Israel shall neither slumber nor sleep" (Psalm 121:4–5 KJV). God loves you and watches over you to keep you safe from harm and to turn away calamities and vexations. And because He's omnipotent and eternal, He's well able to guard you. Nothing slips by Him. He never nods off for a few moments. The Lord is set on protecting you; He's all-powerful, and His eyes are always wide open for any danger.

SPIRITUAL REST

Like many people today, you may be "heavy laden," working long hours at a demanding job and saddled by concerns and anxieties. The good news is you can find relief in Jesus. He promises:

Come unto me, all ye that labour and are heavy laden, and I will give you rest. Take my yoke upon you, and learn of me; for I am meek and lowly in heart: and ye shall find rest unto your souls. For my yoke is easy, and my burden is light.
MATTHEW 11:28–30 KJV

"Come to me, all you who are weary and burdened, and I will give you rest. Take my yoke upon you and learn from me, for I am gentle and humble in heart, and you will find rest for your souls. For my yoke is easy and my burden is light."
MATTHEW 11:28–30 NIV

Isaiah 53:4 (NLT) says, "It was our weaknesses he carried; it was our sorrows that weighed him down." Jesus took the burden of your sin and sorrow upon Himself. You still must bear a yoke to do His work, and there will be burdens to carry, but they're light.

PEACE AMID TRIBULATION

Jesus had just told His disciples, "You will grieve, but your grief will turn to joy. . . . Now is your time of grief, but I will see you again and you will rejoice, and no one will take away your joy" (John 16:20, 22 NIV). Then He said:

> *These things I have spoken unto you, that in me ye might have peace. In the world ye shall have tribulation: but be of good cheer; I have overcome the world.*
>
> JOHN 16:33 KJV

> *"I have told you these things, so that in me you may have peace. In this world you will have trouble. But take heart! I have overcome the world."*
>
> JOHN 16:33 NIV

If the Spirit of Jesus Christ dwells in you and you walk in His Spirit, then you will experience the peace He has promised. This is not to say that you won't have trouble—because as long as you live in this world, you'll face problems. But you can be cheerful through it all, knowing that Jesus has overcome the world. Because His Spirit dwells in you, you too can overcome the world.

GUARDIAN ANGELS

The verse below is often quoted to describe the ministry of God's angels, but when the Bible speaks of "the angel of the LORD," it refers specifically to the theophany (God-body) that the Lord Himself takes on when He appears to people. So this verse is saying that God is personally around you to protect you. But this statement is also true of rank-and-file angels, so it's valid to quote it in that context. As Psalm 91:9–11 makes clear, when God sends His angels to guard you, He Himself is protecting you.

The angel of the LORD encampeth round about them that fear him, and delivereth them.
PSALM 34:7 KJV

The angel of the LORD encamps around those who fear him, and he delivers them.
PSALM 34:7 NIV

When you face great danger or anxiety, you'll be glad that you memorized this verse. Quoting it will bring you comfort and remind you of the Lord's faithfulness to keep you from danger. Think of a camp of angels with multitudes of tents and warriors that have set up a protective barrier around you.

GOD DELIVERS THE RIGHTEOUS

In the verse below, God makes a very reassuring promise: If you're doing your best to love and obey the Lord, He will deliver you from all your troubles when you cry out to Him. He may not deliver you as quickly as you wish or in the exact manner you'd hoped, but He will deliver you from every problem.

The righteous cry, and the LORD heareth,
and delivereth them out of all their troubles.
PSALM 34:17 KJV

The righteous cry out, and the LORD hears them;
he delivers them from all their troubles.
PSALM 34:17 NIV

Of course, God may not deliver you from certain ongoing financial problems, chronic illnesses, or other troubles until you arrive in heaven. In Luke 6:20–22, Jesus described people living in poverty, suffering hunger, and being despised and said that they would be rewarded and comforted in God's eternal kingdom—not before. But take heart! God will frequently deliver you from problems and troubles in the here and now. One way or the other, He will make things right.

THE BATTLE IS GOD'S

In the days when Jehoshaphat was king, the combined armies of Moab, Edom, and Ammon invaded Judah. Jehoshaphat and the people gathered to fast and pray, and after Jehoshaphat cried out to God, a Levite named Jahaziel stood and prophesied:

Thus saith the LORD unto you, Be not afraid
nor dismayed by reason of this great multitude;
for the battle is not yours, but God's.
2 CHRONICLES 20:15 KJV

"This is what the LORD says to you: 'Do not be
afraid or discouraged because of this vast army.
For the battle is not yours, but God's.'"
2 CHRONICLES 20:15 NIV

Encouraged, Jehoshaphat's army marched out to meet the invaders, and because he believed God's promise, the king sent musicians and singers in front of his army to praise the Lord and proclaim that He was about to give them victory. And God did a miracle! He caused the invaders to attack one another, and when the men of Judah came upon them, the enemy soldiers were already dead. God still says today, "Do not be afraid. . .for the battle is not yours, but God's."

A VERY PRESENT HELP

Proverbs 18:10 (NASB) says, "The name of the LORD is a strong tower; the righteous runs into it and is safe." Many verses in the Bible state that God is your high rock, your strong fortress, or your strong tower. These are all fortified places designed as refuges in times of war. Like Masada in the desert of southern Israel, for example, the Jews have always had impregnable fortresses, perched atop isolated crags, to which they could flee. They were a refuge when all other defenses had been overrun. The following verse tells us who our refuge is today:

God is our refuge and strength,
a very present help in trouble.
PSALM 46:1 KJV

God is our refuge and strength,
an ever-present help in trouble.
PSALM 46:1 NIV

The appeal of this verse is the statement that God is "an ever-present help in trouble." His unassailable defenses are close at hand during life's tests and difficulties—unlike Jewish fortresses in remote locations. So you never need fear having the enemy overwhelm and overrun you. God is only a few short steps away when you need His protection the most.

DON'T BE DISMAYED

The verse below opens with a very encouraging statement: "Fear thou not; for I am with thee." God wants you to know that although your circumstances may be frightening, He is with you in all His power to protect you. Note also that He says, "Be not dismayed." To be dismayed means "to cause to lose courage or resolution because of alarm or fear." When you're about to cave in with fear or discouragement, remember: God has promised to help you and uphold you.

Fear thou not; for I am with thee: be not dismayed; for I am thy God: I will strengthen thee; yea, I will help thee; yea, I will uphold thee with the right hand of my righteousness.
Isaiah 41:10 KJV

"So do not fear, for I am with you; do not be dismayed, for I am your God. I will strengthen you and help you; I will uphold you with my righteous right hand."
Isaiah 41:10 NIV

Many Christians down through the ages have drawn great encouragement from this verse. When you're facing troubling times and need encouragement, you'll be glad you memorized it.

MOMENT OF TRUTH

The Jews throughout the Persian Empire were in danger of being exterminated, so Mordecai told Esther that likely the reason God had made her queen of Persia was so she could use her position to petition the king. But God wasn't limited to using Esther. She was His first choice, but if she feared to take a stand, God would still find a way to save the Jews—but she'd suffer for her disobedience:

For if thou altogether holdest thy peace at this time, then shall there enlargement and deliverance arise to the Jews from another place; but thou and thy father's house shall be destroyed: and who knoweth whether thou art come to the kingdom for such a time as this?
ESTHER 4:14 KJV

"For if you remain silent at this time, relief and deliverance for the Jews will arise from another place, but you and your father's family will perish. And who knows but that you have come to your royal position for such a time as this?"
ESTHER 4:14 NIV

When your moment of truth comes, have the courage to take a stand.

LET GOD FIGHT FOR YOU

Sometimes you'll face insurmountable troubles, ones you can't resolve with your own strength and wisdom. This was the situation the Israelites encountered after leaving Egypt: A chariot army was racing toward them, and they were trapped against the Red Sea. They couldn't do a thing! Then God told them to be perfectly still. *He* was going to do everything that needed to be done. And He did. He parted the Red Sea, allowing His people to escape, then sent the waters crashing down over the Egyptian chariot army, drowning them.

The LORD shall fight for you, and ye shall hold your peace.
EXODUS 14:14 KJV

"The LORD will fight for you; you need only to be still."
EXODUS 14:14 NIV

It can be very difficult to hold your peace and be still when the urge to do something—anything!—overwhelms you. But it's in moments like that when you quietly wait for the Lord so that He has the space and the opportunity to do a miracle—to make a way where there is no way.

GOING FORTH IN GOD'S NAME

The verse below is from a wholehearted prayer by King Asa. The Cushites were a people from modern Sudan, south of Egypt, and when Asa heard the alarming news that a vast army of them was invading Judah, he prayed:

LORD, it is nothing with thee to help, whether with many,
or with them that have no power: help us, O LORD our God;
for we rest on thee, and in thy name we go against this multitude.
O LORD, thou art our God; let no man prevail against thee.
2 CHRONICLES 14:11 KJV

"LORD, there is no one like you to help the powerless
against the mighty. Help us, LORD our God,
for we rely on you, and in your name we have come
against this vast army. LORD, you are our God;
do not let mere mortals prevail against you."
2 CHRONICLES 14:11 NIV

Did God answer this prayer? Yes, He did: "The LORD struck down the Cushites before Asa and Judah. . . . Such a great number of Cushites fell that they could not recover; they were crushed before the LORD and his forces" (2 Chronicles 14:12–13 NIV).

VICTORY IN ANY SITUATION

In this brief verse, Paul specifically addresses his ability to be victorious and manage to get by, both when he suffered financial lack and when he enjoyed prosperity. Many Christians, however, quote this verse when they face many other kinds of difficult situations. When you're bewildered and overwhelmed by a task you don't feel equal to, or when you're dealing with a problem you've never faced before, this verse assures you that with Christ strengthening you, you have the ability to handle "all things":

I can do all things through Christ which strengtheneth me.
PHILIPPIANS 4:13 KJV

I can do all this through him who gives me strength.
PHILIPPIANS 4:13 NIV

This is such an inclusive statement that it automatically answers the question "But what about this situation? Can God help me there?" The answer has already been given. Yes, with the Spirit of Christ strengthening you, you can do "all things."

WITH JESUS' HELP

Paul said in Philippians 4:13 (KJV), "I can do *all things* through Christ" (emphasis added). But the reverse is also true. In the verse below, Jesus pointed out, "Apart from me you can do *nothing*":

Abide in me, and I in you. As the branch cannot bear fruit of itself, except it abide in the vine; no more can ye, except ye abide in me. I am the vine, ye are the branches: He that abideth in me, and I in him, the same bringeth forth much fruit: for without me ye can do nothing.
JOHN 15:4–5 KJV

"Remain in me, as I also remain in you. No branch can bear fruit by itself; it must remain in the vine. Neither can you bear fruit unless you remain in me. I am the vine; you are the branches. If you remain in me and I in you, you will bear much fruit; apart from me you can do nothing."
JOHN 15:4–5 NIV

You can do nothing of lasting spiritual value without Jesus. God doesn't expect you to produce good works on your own. Only by dwelling in Jesus do you receive His grace to do good works.

THE LORD ALMIGHTY

In Jeremiah 32:27 (KJV), God asks, "Behold, I am the LORD, the God of all flesh: is there any thing too hard for me?" This memory verse, spoken by the prophet Jeremiah, provides the answer:

Ah Lord GOD! behold, thou hast made the heaven and the earth by thy great power and stretched out arm, and there is nothing too hard for thee.
JEREMIAH 32:17 KJV

"Ah, Sovereign LORD, you have made the heavens and the earth by your great power and outstretched arm. Nothing is too hard for you."
JEREMIAH 32:17 NIV

The Bible informs God's people of how great His power is when it reminds them that He created the entire world and everything in it. Furthermore, He formed all the galaxies in the entire universe: "By the word of the LORD the heavens were made, their starry host by the breath of his mouth" (Psalm 33:6 NIV). When you're facing an impossible situation and need God to do a miracle, these verses ought to encourage your faith.

STRENGTH IN JOY

It would hardly seem that something as simple as joy could keep you going when you're beaten down and ready to give up. But if you keep your mind on the Lord and His promises, His joy will breathe courage into you. Peter had just finished telling his readers about heaven when he said, "In this you *greatly rejoice*, even though now for a little while. . .you have been distressed by various trials" (1 Peter 1:6 NASB, emphasis added). Understood in this light, the following memory verse, though short, is extremely powerful:

Neither be ye sorry; for the joy of
the LORD is your strength.
NEHEMIAH 8:10 KJV

"Do not grieve, for the joy of the
LORD is your strength."
NEHEMIAH 8:10 NIV

The Psalms declare, "Be glad in the LORD and rejoice" (32:11 NKJV), and in an emphatic declaration, Paul wrote, "Rejoice in the Lord always. Again I will say, rejoice!" (Philippians 4:4 NKJV). If you wondered why the Bible writers continually emphasized "rejoicing in the Lord," now you know. His joy gives strength.

GOD IS TRUSTWORTHY

Throughout the Bible, you can read how God has made many, many promises to His people, and because you are His son, these promises are yours. People may make promises and intend to keep them but are not always able to due to circumstances beyond their control. But there are never circumstances beyond God's control. The verse below asks two questions that bring out how trustworthy God is:

God is not a man, that he should lie; neither the son of man, that he should repent: hath he said, and shall he not do it? or hath he spoken, and shall he not make it good?
NUMBERS 23:19 KJV

"God is not human, that he should lie, not a human being, that he should change his mind. Does he speak and then not act? Does he promise and not fulfill?"
NUMBERS 23:19 NIV

God is fully aware of the facts and circumstances when He makes you a promise. He understands that things may look desperate when it comes time to make good on His promises—but He saw that difficulty back when He first made them, and it didn't stop Him from promising.

PERSEVERANCE AND HOPE

Sometimes life situations can become so difficult that you feel like you're at the point of fainting. While it's wonderful to know that there will be no more stress, lack, and conflicts when you get to heaven, often you may be desperate for relief in the here and now. Here, David emphasizes the importance of trusting the Lord to show His mercy and goodness in this life:

I had fainted, unless I had believed to see the goodness
of the LORD in the land of the living.
PSALM 27:13 KJV

I remain confident of this: I will see the goodness
of the LORD in the land of the living.
PSALM 27:13 NIV

In the NIV, David clearly states that the Lord will show him kindness in this life. So which translation is the most accurate? It could be either. The 1995 edition of the NASB translates it: "I would have despaired unless I had believed that I would see the goodness of the LORD in the land of the living," but its footnotes mention that the verse could start by saying, "Surely I believed. . ." So it works both ways.

HARVEST IS COMING

Being a disciple can be difficult. Jesus said, "If any man will come after me, let him deny himself. . . . For whosoever will save his life shall lose it: and whosoever will lose his life for my sake shall find it" (Matthew 16:24–25 KJV). But "losing your life" is difficult, and some days you may feel like a dieter on a strict diet—it's just too hard and isn't worth it. The Bible has an answer to that:

And let us not be weary in well doing:
for in due season we shall reap, if we faint not.
GALATIANS 6:9 KJV

Let us not become weary in doing good, for at the proper
time we will reap a harvest if we do not give up.
GALATIANS 6:9 NIV

Like a dieter trying to reach a target weight, you need to keep your eyes on the goal. If you can hold out and persist in doing good, it will be worth the sacrifice. Harvest doesn't come for a while, not until "due season," so you need some fortitude to delay your gratification. So don't lose hope and faint. Keep believing and following God! The reward is worth the wait.

STRATEGY AGAINST TEMPTATION

Memorizing the verse below will remind you of the solution to one of life's most constant problems—at least for many men: the tendency to look with longing on attractive women. Job realized that unless he came up with a strategy ahead of time, when he found himself ambushed by the sight of a sexually attractive woman, he would be tempted to lust. So he came up with a plan:

I made a covenant with mine eyes;
why then should I think upon a maid?
Job 31:1 KJV

"I made a covenant with my eyes not to
look lustfully at a young woman."
Job 31:1 NIV

Job had already worked out what his response would be: He would refuse to even let his gaze linger on a beautiful maiden. He put his eyes on notice that they must look away before he could be tempted. Solomon advised, "Don't lust for her beauty. Don't let her coy glances seduce you" (Proverbs 6:25 NLT). The best way to avoid being seduced is to look the other way before the temptation arrives.

SPIRITUAL AND MENTAL ADULTERY

Jesus didn't present a new concept in the verse below. In the Ten Commandments, God said, "You shall not covet [that is, selfishly desire and attempt to acquire]. . .your neighbor's wife" (Exodus 20:17 AMP). Coveting involved more than just a casual glance; it was a prolonged, deliberate look of desire and scheming to sleep with another man's wife.

Ye have heard that it was said by them of old time,
Thou shalt not commit adultery: but I say unto you,
That whosoever looketh on a woman to lust after her hath
committed adultery with her already in his heart.
MATTHEW 5:27–28 KJV

"You have heard that it was said, 'You shall not commit adultery.'
But I tell you that anyone who looks at a woman lustfully
has already committed adultery with her in his heart."
MATTHEW 5:27–28 NIV

This is what Jesus referred to when He mentioned "anyone who looks at a woman lustfully." It's not a sin to glance at a beautiful woman and have a sudden sexual thought cross your mind. The sin is succumbing to that desire and continuing to look at her and fantasize about her.

FLEE FORNICATION

Solomon describes a naive young man: "He was crossing the street near the house of an immoral woman, strolling down the path by her house. . . . So she seduced him. . . . He followed her at once, like an ox going to the slaughter" (Proverbs 7:8, 21–22 NLT). The young man's first mistake was "strolling down the path by her house." He knew she gave sexual favors to the town's young men and was seeking her. His next mistake was not running away before she opened her mouth and tempted him. Sexual temptation can be intense and nearly overpowering. Don't underestimate it. The Bible commands:

Flee fornication.
1 CORINTHIANS 6:18 KJV

Flee from sexual immorality.
1 CORINTHIANS 6:18 NIV

Potiphar's wife was an immoral woman also, but instead of "strolling down the path by her house," Joseph "kept out of her way as much as possible." She finally managed to get alone with him, seized his cloak, and insisted, "Come on, sleep with me!" but "Joseph tore himself away" and "ran from the house" (Genesis 39:10, 12 NLT). You must put physical distance between yourself and sexual temptation.

OVERCOMING TEMPTATION

Sometimes you're subjected to strong, relentless temptations, and you may feel that it's only a matter of time before you cave in. It could be a diet-destroying lust for a pastry, a burning desire for illicit sex, or the impulse to buy something you can't afford. But Paul had this to say about overcoming temptation:

There hath no temptation taken you but such as is common to man: but God is faithful, who will not suffer you to be tempted above that ye are able; but will with the temptation also make a way to escape, that ye may be able to bear it.
1 Corinthians 10:13 kjv

No temptation has overtaken you except what is common to mankind. And God is faithful; he will not let you be tempted beyond what you can bear. But when you are tempted, he will also provide a way out so that you can endure it.
1 Corinthians 10:13 niv

Pray and ask God for strategies on how to cope with temptation—whether they involve written reminders, avoiding certain places, or filling your mind with scriptures on the subject. Pray, and do your part, and God will strengthen you and help you resist temptation.

GRACE WITH A BACKBONE

The same grace of God that lovingly, gently forgives you for all your sins and brings you salvation also teaches you to have a strong moral backbone and say no to ungodly behavior. Many people think God's grace is so mild-mannered that it sweetly overlooks sin in believers' lives and blushingly sweeps their moral failures under the rug. This simply isn't the case:

For the grace of God that bringeth salvation hath appeared to all men, teaching us that, denying ungodliness and worldly lusts, we should live soberly, righteously, and godly, in this present world.
TITUS 2:11–12 KJV

For the grace of God has appeared that offers salvation to all people. It teaches us to say "No" to ungodliness and worldly passions, and to live self-controlled, upright and godly lives in this present age.
TITUS 2:11–12 NIV

The same grace of God that brings you salvation also gives you the oomph to overcome temptation, take a determined stand for righteousness, and make hard moral choices in the midst of a depraved and decadent society.

BE VIGILANT

Some people find this imagery baffling. Amos 3:4 (NKJV) asks, "Will a lion roar in the forest, when he has no prey?" No, as long as a lion is hunting for prey, it remains silent. Only when it is fed will it roar. So why does Peter say that "the devil prowls around like a roaring lion"? Well, just because the lion is known for roaring doesn't mean he's roaring when he's on the prowl. After all, if you could hear where he was, you wouldn't have to be so vigilant.

Be sober, be vigilant; because your adversary the devil, as a roaring lion, walketh about, seeking whom he may devour.
1 PETER 5:8 KJV

Be alert and of sober mind. Your enemy the devil prowls around like a roaring lion looking for someone to devour.
1 PETER 5:8 NIV

The devil prowls around looking for Christians who are spiritually asleep, aren't alert, and not paying attention to signs of danger. He roars out of ambush, takes them down, and devours them. Don't let this be you! Be alert. See the devil sneaking up, face him down, resist him. . .and he will flee (see James 4:7).

DEFEATING THE DEVIL

The meaning of the verse below is clearer in the NIV than in the KJV. I had read this verse countless times in my KJV Bible for nearly two decades, but it never impacted me. But when I read it in an NIV Bible, it spoke to me. I immediately decided to memorize it—making it one of my few NIV memory verses. And it has helped me many times.

But the Lord is faithful, who shall stablish you,
and keep you from evil.
2 THESSALONIANS 3:3 KJV

But the Lord is faithful, and he will strengthen
you and protect you from the evil one.
2 THESSALONIANS 3:3 NIV

Very likely the reason this verse stood out to me in the NIV was because in the KJV, the verse speaks of God keeping believers from a vague, general evil, whereas in the NIV, it speaks of God protecting you "from the evil one"—the devil himself, a malignant enemy who personally, willfully seeks to attack and destroy believers. As such, this verse is the answer to the scenario described in 1 Peter 5:8.

RESISTING THE DEVIL

This passage has served like a great shield to many Christians experiencing spiritual attack. The previous promise stated that God would strengthen you and protect you from the evil one, but you have a part to play also. You are to "resist the devil," and James promises that if you do this, "he will flee from you":

Submit yourselves therefore to God.
Resist the devil, and he will flee from you.
James 4:7 KJV

Submit yourselves, then, to God.
Resist the devil, and he will flee from you.
James 4:7 NIV

This may happen quickly, or it may take a while, with you steadfastly resisting the enemy for some time until the moment he buckles under the strain and flees. Note also that this verse states, "Submit yourselves therefore to God." In order to gain power, you must persevere in prayer, continually submitting to God's will. Often the reason that you're under spiritual attack in the first place is because you're resisting God in some area. But when you yield to God, He will protect you fully from the devil.

LOVE CASTS OUT FEAR

This is a powerful promise: "Perfect love casteth out fear." But what precisely is it talking about? Well, two verses previously, the Bible declared, "God is love" (1 John 4:16 KJV). This means that if you live in God and He lives in you, you'll be filled with His love and perfected "in love." Then you'll have "boldness [confidence] in the day of judgment" (verse 17 KJV).

There is no fear in love; but perfect love casteth out fear: because fear hath torment. He that feareth is not made perfect in love.
1 JOHN 4:18 KJV

There is no fear in love. But perfect love drives out fear, because fear has to do with punishment. The one who fears is not made perfect in love.
1 JOHN 4:18 NIV

When you're filled with God's love, you no longer feel fearful that He will reject you. You're confident that He's on your side; you no longer worry that you'll be punished for your sins. This confidence fills you with the positive attitude you need to face life's problems. Be filled with God's perfect love today, and it will cast all fear from your heart.

DESTROYING SATAN'S WORKS

This is a simple but powerful message: The whole reason the Son of God became flesh and came to the earth was so He could demolish the wicked devices of the devil. Jesus seeks to undo every evil thing the devil has done. The Bible states, "God anointed Jesus of Nazareth with the Holy Ghost and with power: [He] went about doing good, and healing all that were oppressed of the devil" (Acts 10:38 KJV) and that God has "delivered us from the power of darkness and conveyed us into the kingdom of the Son of His love" (Colossians 1:13 NKJV). The following memory verse puts it simply:

For this purpose the Son of God was manifested,
that he might destroy the works of the devil.
1 JOHN 3:8 KJV

The reason the Son of God appeared
was to destroy the devil's work.
1 JOHN 3:8 NIV

The Spirit of Jesus is working in the world right now to bring the wicked to repentance, restore ruined lives, heal the sick, and redeem the sinful. And one day He will conquer the final enemy, death, and bring immortality to a rejuvenated new earth.

OVERCOMING THE WORLD

Jesus said, "In the world you will have tribulation; but be of good cheer, I have overcome the world" (John 16:33 NKJV). Is it any wonder, then, that He has promised that, with the Spirit of Jesus living in your heart, you too have overcome this evil world—even though, at the present time, it is causing you tribulation?

Ye are of God, little children, and have overcome them: because greater is he that is in you, than he that is in the world.
1 JOHN 4:4 KJV

You, dear children, are from God and have overcome them, because the one who is in you is greater than the one who is in the world.
1 JOHN 4:4 NIV

This isn't something you can muster up in your own strength. You can be overcoming the world even though it's persecuting you, trampling you underfoot, and making you feel defeated. That's because you *will* one day overcome it. Paul said, "Yet in all these things we are *more* than conquerors through Him who loved us" (Romans 8:37 NKJV, emphasis added). Think of that!

LIGHT AND STRENGTH

The memory verse below is a very beautiful and powerful passage of scripture. The first short phrase is especially poignant: "The Lord is my light." Elsewhere, David said, "For thou art my lamp, O Lord: and the Lord will lighten my darkness" (2 Samuel 22:29 KJV). The patriarch Job spoke of a time "when by his light I walked through darkness" (Job 29:3 KJV). Today's memory verse states:

The Lord is my light and my salvation;
whom shall I fear? the Lord is the strength
of my life; of whom shall I be afraid?
Psalm 27:1 KJV

The Lord is my light and my salvation—
whom shall I fear? The Lord is the stronghold
of my life—of whom shall I be afraid?
Psalm 27:1 NIV

Twice in this short verse, David asked whom he should fear, since God was on his side. David was keenly aware of the Lord's power, so he fully trusted Him to protect him. He declared that God was "the strength of [his] life." The NIV words state this differently, declaring that God was his stronghold. Picture a fortress of strength that completely surrounds you.

PROTECTED BY ANGEL ARMIES

Many Christians believe that every person has two guardian angels. The Bible doesn't give a number, but when it speaks of believing children, it refers to "their angels" (Matthew 18:10). At least one angel guards you (Psalm 34:7), and sometimes there are several (Psalm 91:11). When you're on an important mission, sometimes an army of angels surrounds you! Elisha and Gehazi were in Dothan when an Aramean army surrounded the city. Gehazi was dismayed and asked what they could do. But Elisha wasn't worried:

And he answered, Fear not: for they that be with us are more than they that be with them.
2 KINGS 6:16 KJV

"Don't be afraid," the prophet answered. "Those who are with us are more than those who are with them."
2 KINGS 6:16 NIV

God then opened Gehazi's eyes so he could see into the spiritual realm, and he realized that the hillside around Elisha was filled with blazing horses and chariots of fire—an entire army of angels, more numerous even than the Aramean soldiers on the ground. Not only were there many angels, but they were glowing with great power.

KNOWING AND OBEYING

The verse below is worth memorizing because if you do; the Holy Spirit will probably bring it to your remembrance many times. In the KJV, Jesus says, "If ye know these things"—but He's clearly assuming that His disciples do know these truths. The only question is, Will they do them? The NIV is more straightforward; it simply states when you're aware of these spiritual truths, it's your responsibility to obey them.

If ye know these things, happy are ye if ye do them.
JOHN 13:17 KJV

"Now that you know these things,
you will be blessed if you do them."
JOHN 13:17 NIV

This is strikingly similar to the point of Jesus' parable about the difference between building on solid rock and on shifting sand. He taught, "Anyone who listens to my teaching and follows it is wise, like a person who builds a house on solid rock. . . . But anyone who hears my teaching and doesn't obey it is foolish, like a person who builds a house on sand" (Matthew 7:24, 26 NLT).

WHAT GOD REQUIRES

The Law of Moses contained some harsh regulations, such as "eye for eye" (Leviticus 24:20), but it must be remembered that its end purpose was to safeguard the rights of the common people—in particular the poor, the widows, and orphans. God wanted His people to act justly, to love mercy instead of vengeance, and to realize their own shortcomings, so that they'd look to God to have mercy on them and, in turn, have mercy on others. Thus today's memory verse:

> *He hath shewed thee, O man, what is good; and what doth the LORD require of thee, but to do justly, and to love mercy, and to walk humbly with thy God?*
> MICAH 6:8 KJV

> *He has shown you, O mortal, what is good. And what does the LORD require of you? To act justly and to love mercy and to walk humbly with your God.*
> MICAH 6:8 NIV

You must love both justice and mercy—neither tolerating evil nor seeking revenge. This requires you to walk close to God and to know when to insist on justice and when to extend mercy. This takes genuine humility.

FOLLOWING GOD

Many people are undecided, unsure of whether or not to give their hearts to Christ. They know that Jesus has promised them peace and eternal life, but they also know that following Him is a serious commitment that requires deep changes. So they stall. Other people give their hearts to Christ but later drift away, and God calls them to recommit themselves. Many centuries ago, Elijah challenged the Israelites who were wavering between worshipping the true God and Baal:

> *How long halt ye between two opinions? if the* Lord *be God, follow him: but if Baal, then follow him.*
> 1 Kings 18:21 kjv

> *"How long will you waver between two opinions? If the* Lord *is God, follow him; but if Baal is God, follow him."*
> 1 Kings 18:21 niv

The people didn't answer. They couldn't make up their minds. Now, it's good to give careful thought when making important decisions, and to check out the gospel's claims carefully (Acts 17:11–12). But there comes a time when you must commit yourself. Quoting this verse to yourself can remind you of this principle.

TIME TO FOLLOW

Peter and Andrew were fishermen. They had met Jesus along the Jordan River (John 1:40–42) in the fall of AD 26. Together with their partners, James and John, they followed Jesus throughout Galilee for several months. In the summer of AD 27 they were again in Capernaum, and they returned to fishing. Then Jesus decided to do another tour of Galilee, so He called Peter and Andrew, then James and John, to follow Him full-time.

And he saith unto them, Follow me,
and I will make you fishers of men.
MATTHEW 4:19 KJV

"Come, follow me," Jesus said,
"and I will send you out to fish for people."
MATTHEW 4:19 NIV

Some people think Jesus was a total stranger to the fishermen when He called them to drop what they were doing and follow Him. But they knew Jesus well, having followed Him previously while learning from His teaching. You too have probably spent ample time with Jesus. You've had time to consider serving Him. So if He calls you into full-time ministry—or on a short-term mission or other type of service—will you drop what you're doing and follow?

DON'T BE ASHAMED OF JESUS

A number of Christians are uneasy with some of Jesus' teachings and frankly wish He hadn't said them. Or they dismiss them as simplistic. Jesus warned His disciples not to be ashamed of Him or of His teachings:

> *For what shall it profit a man, if he shall gain the whole world, and lose his own soul? Or what shall a man give in exchange for his soul? Whosoever therefore shall be ashamed of me and of my words in this adulterous and sinful generation; of him also shall the Son of man be ashamed, when he cometh in the glory of his Father with the holy angels.*
>
> Mark 8:36–38 KJV

> *"What good is it for someone to gain the whole world, yet forfeit their soul? Or what can anyone give in exchange for their soul? If anyone is ashamed of me and my words in this adulterous and sinful generation, the Son of Man will be ashamed of them when he comes in his Father's glory with the holy angels."*
>
> Mark 8:36–38 NIV

These may be strong verses, but they're worth memorizing because they remind you never to lose respect for Jesus and His words.

SAVE YOUR LIFE OR LOSE IT

Jesus often turned conventional logic on its head. He said the first would be last, that they who made themselves slaves of all would be rulers, and that they who humbled themselves would be exalted. But Jesus' teachings actually make good sense. Here He states the startling words that any man who saves his life will lose it, but he who loses his life will save it:

If any man will come after me, let him deny himself, and take up his cross daily, and follow me. For whosoever will save his life shall lose it: but whosoever will lose his life for my sake, the same shall save it.
LUKE 9:23–24 KJV

"Whoever wants to be my disciple must deny themselves and take up their cross daily and follow me. For whoever wants to save their life will lose it, but whoever loses their life for me will save it."
LUKE 9:23–24 NIV

Jesus explained this conundrum when He compared His followers to grains of wheat that had to "die" and be buried in order to bring forth life (John 12:24; see also 1 Corinthians 15:36–38).

UNCONDITIONAL SURRENDER

In the verse below, Jesus stated a requirement for discipleship. The context for this verse is two parables. In the first, Jesus described a man about to build a tower but who was advised that he "sit down first and *count the cost*, whether he has enough to finish it" (Luke 14:28 NKJV, emphasis added). The cost of following Jesus is high, and it's best to know that going in.

So likewise, whosoever he be of you that forsaketh not all that he hath, he cannot be my disciple.
LUKE 14:33 KJV

"In the same way, those of you who do not give up everything you have cannot be my disciples."
LUKE 14:33 NIV

In the second parable, Jesus described a king with ten thousand soldiers about to battle a king with twenty thousand. Jesus said that the first king had to decide whether he could win. If not, he needed to send a delegation to the other king and seek terms of surrender (verses 31–32). If you wish to be Jesus' disciple, know this: He requires unconditional surrender. You must relinquish all your rights.

THE TRUTH SETS YOU FREE

To truly follow Christ, it's not enough to give your heart to Him then live your life however you please, indifferent to His requirements. It may be enough to save you, but it won't make you a disciple. Here, Jesus states the condition for being His disciple:

> *Then said Jesus to those Jews which believed on him, If ye continue in my word, then are ye my disciples indeed; and ye shall know the truth, and the truth shall make you free.*
> JOHN 8:31–32 KJV

> *To the Jews who had believed him, Jesus said, "If you hold to my teaching, you are really my disciples. Then you will know the truth, and the truth will set you free."*
> JOHN 8:31–32 NIV

Jesus said, "If ye continue in my word, then are ye my disciples indeed." You may think you're losing out by becoming His servant; you may wonder if committing to obey Him will cause you to miss out on life. But Jesus said that it's actually the path to freedom. He promised, "If the Son makes you free, you shall be free indeed" (John 8:36 NKJV).

PROOF OF THE LORD'S LOVE

When God rebukes you for a wrong attitude or disciplines you for your disobedience, you can get the feeling that He's angry with you and judging you. You can then feel discouraged and ready to give up. He may be upset, true, but He isn't *judging* you. He's disciplining you, and according to the dictionary, discipline is "the practice of training people to obey rules or a code of behavior, using punishment to correct disobedience." Jesus says:

As many as I love, I rebuke and chasten:
be zealous therefore, and repent.
REVELATION 3:19 KJV

"Those whom I love I rebuke and discipline.
So be earnest and repent."
REVELATION 3:19 NIV

When the Lord disciplines you, it's proof that He loves you, not that He's fed up with you and about to throw you out. It shows that He's invested in you and cares enough about you to try to improve you. Knowing that He loves you and is disciplining you for your own good should motivate you to repent, which shows your love for Him.

WHEN GOD GRIEVES YOU

God realizes that when He chastises you, it often causes you grief. Despite the fact that He knows you will benefit from discipline, it doesn't give Him pleasure to administer it. God doesn't even take pleasure in judging evil people but says, "I take no pleasure in the death of the wicked, but rather that the wicked turn from his way and live" (Ezekiel 33:11 NASB). How much more does He feel *our* pain!

But though he cause grief, yet will he have compassion according to the multitude of his mercies. For he doth not afflict willingly nor grieve the children of men.
LAMENTATIONS 3:32–33 KJV

Though he brings grief, he will show compassion, so great is his unfailing love. For he does not willingly bring affliction or grief to anyone.
LAMENTATIONS 3:32–33 NIV

God will always be gentle and loving to you after you've endured His discipline: "May the God of all grace, who called us to His eternal glory by Christ Jesus, *after you have suffered a while*, perfect, establish, strengthen, and settle you" (1 Peter 5:10 NKJV, emphasis added).

AFFLICTION CORRECTS YOU

The author of Psalm 119, probably writing during the days of the Persian Empire, was most likely an impoverished but pious scribe living in Judea. He was not only poor, but he was often mocked and persecuted by the corrupt rich. In addition, he frequently suffered physical afflictions. He recognized the hand of God in all his hardships, however, and was even thankful for his bouts of poor health, saying:

Before I was afflicted I went astray:
but now have I kept thy word.
Psalm 119:67 KJV

Before I was afflicted I went astray,
but now I obey your word.
Psalm 119:67 NIV

Paul declared, "I am exceedingly joyful in all our tribulation" (2 Corinthians 7:4 NKJV), and he also rejoiced in his troubles and looked on the bright side: His prolonged afflictions caused him to return to the Lord, to study His Word more fervently, and to obey it diligently. This will often be the case in your life as well. God allows you to experience suffering because He knows it will cause you to repent and love Him and His Word even more (see Psalm 119:71).

GLORIOUS FUTURE REVEALED

In New Testament times, Christians often suffered persecution. The apostles didn't make light of what believers were going through. They acknowledged what brave men and women were enduring. But difficult as it sometimes was, Paul assured them that such suffering couldn't compare to the glorious rewards that God had in store for them.

For I reckon that the sufferings of this present time are not worthy to be compared with the glory which shall be revealed in us.
ROMANS 8:18 KJV

I consider that our present sufferings are not worth comparing with the glory that will be revealed in us.
ROMANS 8:18 NIV

Paul spoke of "the glory that will be revealed in us," so this is referring to more than celestial gardens, crystal-gold mansions, and fountains of living water. This speaks of a glorious change in your own body—to where you shine with the light of the Spirit. The Bible further states, "Then shall the righteous shine forth as the sun in the kingdom of their Father" (Matthew 13:43 KJV), and you will "forget your misery, and remember it as waters that have passed away" (Job 11:16 NKJV).

GOD BRINGS ABOUT GOOD

The verse below is a favorite for memorization for many Christians because it offers real hope when bad things happen. It also offers the explanation that although you may suffer through disasters, there is more to the picture than just the darkness you're presently seeing. God is all-powerful and eventually will bring good out of *every* situation.

And we know that all things work together for good to them that love God, to them who are the called according to his purpose.
ROMANS 8:28 KJV

And we know that in all things God works for the good of those who love him, who have been called according to his purpose.
ROMANS 8:28 NIV

Note that this verse doesn't say that "all things are good." They're not. Some circumstances are evil and not the Father's desire for you. Rather, it says that "all things *work together* for good." God will get good out of even evil events (see Genesis 50:20). Also, note that this isn't a promise to the world. It's only for God's children "who love him, who have been called according to his purpose."

RECOVERING FROM SETBACKS

Joel's prophetic book describes a punishing locust plague on a vast scale. Every few years, untold millions of locusts hatched in the northern Sahara Desert then swept out in massive waves into the surrounding lands, devouring all plant life. They sometimes invaded Israel and left the land stripped bare. But after this devastating judgment, God had good news:

And I will restore to you the years
that the locust hath eaten.
JOEL 2:25 KJV

"I will repay you for the years
the locusts have eaten."
JOEL 2:25 NIV

In Joel 1:4, God described four separate waves of locusts, and in Joel 2:25, He told the repentant Israelites that He would make up for the loss they suffered. "Shout for joy and rejoice, for the LORD has done great things. . . . He has given you the early rain. . . . The threshing floors will be full of grain. . . . You will have plenty to eat and be satisfied" (Joel 2:21, 23–24, 26 NASB). God is like that with His children today as well, which is why Christians often quote this promise after suffering loss.

AVOID OBSCENITY

Many Christians need a reminder to watch their language. If you hear continual swearing in your workplace, the temptation can be to use a little foul language yourself to be accepted as "one of the guys." Some believers even get pleasure out of an occasional swear-word shocking fellow Christians. They feel they're proving that they're not sanctimonious and religious, that they're in touch with "real people." Whatever their motives for swearing, the Bible says:

Neither filthiness, nor foolish talking, nor jesting,
which are not convenient: but rather giving of thanks.
EPHESIANS 5:4 KJV

Nor should there be obscenity, foolish talk or coarse joking,
which are out of place, but rather thanksgiving.
EPHESIANS 5:4 NIV

It seems the Ephesians had a bit of a problem along these lines, for in this same epistle, Paul wrote, "Don't use foul or abusive language. Let everything you say be good and helpful, so that your words will be an encouragement to those who hear them" (Ephesians 4:29 NLT). Whatever your motivations for swearing, Paul says, "Now is the time to get rid of. . .dirty language" (Colossians 3:8 NLT).

ARISE AND BE DOING

God told David that his son Solomon would build a temple, so the king set aside millions of dollars' worth of gold, silver, bronze, and iron for its construction; quarried great blocks of marble; amassed a huge lumberyard of cedar; organized stonecutters, masons, and carpenters; and even drew up blueprints for it. All Solomon had to do was to build. Thus, David told him:

Arise therefore, and be doing, and the LORD be with thee.
1 CHRONICLES 22:16 KJV

"Now begin the work, and the LORD be with you."
1 CHRONICLES 22:16 NIV

Sometimes, even when you know what you're supposed to do, you get cold feet. It could be that you have a problem with procrastination, or it could be fear. But when you know that it's God's will for you to take on some project, and it's obvious that He will bless it, you can proceed. You may feel like hesitating, but the time for hesitation is over. It's now time to get to work. That's when the above blessing is most appropriate.

GOD'S ABUNDANT PROVISION

John 3:16 (NKJV) says that "God *so* loved the world that He gave His only begotten Son, that whoever believes in Him should not perish but have everlasting life" (emphasis added). Understood in this context, the following question is actually a beautiful promise:

He that spared not his own Son,
but delivered him up for us all, how shall
he not with him also freely give us all things?
ROMANS 8:32 KJV

He who did not spare his own Son,
but gave him up for us all—how will he not also,
along with him, graciously give us all things?
ROMANS 8:32 NIV

This verse primarily describes how God will bless you with an abundant inheritance in heaven, but His blessings also extend to your needs in this life. That is many Christians' focus when quoting this. But three verses later, Paul asks, "Does it mean he no longer loves us if we have trouble or calamity, or are persecuted, or hungry, or destitute?" (Romans 8:35 NLT). Sometimes believers have these problems. But the answer, of course, is that nothing can separate you from Christ's love.

GOD'S ENDLESS SUPPLY

The verse below is one of the most-quoted passages in the Bible. For two thousand years, Christians have claimed it and found God true to His word. Paul wrote it to the disciples of Philippi who, although they were poor and struggling, gave generously to fellow Christians who were suffering even more desperate times. Paul reassured them that God would be certain to see that they themselves didn't lack:

But my God shall supply all your need according to his riches in glory by Christ Jesus.
PHILIPPIANS 4:19 KJV

And my God will meet all your needs according to the riches of his glory in Christ Jesus.
PHILIPPIANS 4:19 NIV

God has an endless supply of everything you need. He owns "the cattle upon a thousand hills" (Psalm 50:10 KJV). In fact, He went on to say, "The *world* is mine, and the fulness thereof" (verse 12, emphasis added). What does the phrase "riches in glory" mean? Some Christians think it's referring to God's "riches in heaven," but calling heaven "glory" is a modern poetic trend. This actually refers to Christ's glory (see John 17:5).

SUCCESS AND PROSPERITY

God wants you to succeed and be prosperous. While you might like most of that success and prosperity to be in the form of financial abundance, this verse isn't a guarantee that you'll become wealthy if you only read and obey your Bible. But God has promised to meet all your needs (Philippians 4:19), and in most cases, if you're obedient, it's reasonable to expect Him to help you earn a good living.

This book of the law shall not depart out of thy mouth;
but thou shalt meditate therein day and night,
that thou mayest observe to do according to all that
is written therein: for then thou shalt make thy way
prosperous, and then thou shalt have good success.
Joshua 1:8 KJV

"Keep this Book of the Law always on your lips; meditate on
it day and night, so that you may be careful to do everything
written in it. Then you will be prosperous and successful."
Joshua 1:8 NIV

May you have success in representing Christ on the earth, and may you prosper in your spiritual, social, and financial spheres.

MATERIALISM AND GREED

It's not a sin to be rich, but possessing great wealth presents several built-in challenges and difficulties. Even desiring to be rich and longing for money is fraught with peril. Paul wrote, "Those who want to get rich fall into temptation and a trap and many foolish and harmful desires which plunge people into ruin and destruction. . . . Some by longing for [money] have wandered away from the faith" (1 Timothy 6:9–10 NASB). Your true life—the inner, spiritual life that God alone gives you—doesn't come from material things.

Take heed, and beware of covetousness: for a man's life consisteth not in the abundance of the things which he possesseth.
LUKE 12:15 KJV

"Watch out! Be on your guard against all kinds of greed; life does not consist in an abundance of possessions."
LUKE 12:15 NIV

Teaching on usefulness for the kingdom of God, Jesus said, "Other seeds fell among thorns that grew up and choked out the tender plants." He explained that this seed "represents those who hear God's word, but. . .the message is crowded out by. . .the lure of wealth" (Matthew 13:7, 22 NLT).

THANKFUL FOR THE BASICS

If you had no need of physical possessions before you entered this world, and will have no need of them after you leave it, then why obsess over material belongings during your short stay on earth? You might as well do as Paul wrote and be content with the simplest necessities—food and clothing:

For we brought nothing into this world, and it is certain we can carry nothing out. And having food and raiment let us be therewith content.
1 Timothy 6:7–8 KJV

For we brought nothing into the world, and we can take nothing out of it. But if we have food and clothing, we will be content with that.
1 Timothy 6:7–8 NIV

Paul traveled from city to city preaching the gospel, so he didn't even include a steady place to live as a need. He said that he had "no certain dwellingplace" (1 Corinthians 4:11 KJV). But for most people, having the security of a home is a basic need. You may sometimes lack the extras that make life enjoyable, but as long as your basic needs are met, you can be thankful.

CONTENT WITHOUT COVETING

The KJV rendering of the verse below needs a little explaining, because these days the word *conversation* refers to people talking to one another. But in King James' day, "conversation" meant "way of life." (Admittedly, for some people talking *is* a way of life.) And "covetousness" means "having a strong desire for material things, especially the belongings of someone else." Only if you overcome covetousness will you be content with what you have. How do you do that? By knowing that the God who cares for your needs is with you and will never leave you.

Let your conversation be without covetousness;
and be content with such things as ye have: for he
hath said, I will never leave thee, nor forsake thee.
HEBREWS 13:5 KJV

Keep your lives free from the love of money and be
content with what you have, because God has said,
"Never will I leave you; never will I forsake you."
HEBREWS 13:5 NIV

It's greatly encouraging to know that God will never abandon you under any circumstances. When you fully grasp this truth, it will help you to loosen your grip on material things and instead hold on to eternal values.

MATERIAL THINGS COME SECOND

Jesus said, "So don't worry about these things, saying, 'What will we eat? What will we drink? What will we wear?'. . . Your heavenly Father already knows all your needs" (Matthew 6:31–32 NLT). God is aware that you need certain things to survive (food, drink, clothing, and shelter) and that it's a serious matter if you lack them. But He will provide. So He counsels you to seek Him first and foremost:

But seek ye first the kingdom of God, and his righteousness;
and all these things shall be added unto you.
MATTHEW 6:33 KJV

"But seek first his kingdom and his righteousness,
and all these things will be given to you as well."
MATTHEW 6:33 NIV

It may seem backward to seek God first when you desperately need food, drink, and clothing. But putting God first shows that you realize that *He* is your source of supply. Yes, you still need to do a day's work to provide your needs, but it's important to "remember the LORD your God, for it is He who gives you power to get wealth" (Deuteronomy 8:18 NKJV).

REJOICING IN DESPERATE TIMES

The following passage describes being joyful in difficult times and praising God even when everything goes wrong. This isn't easy.

Although the fig tree shall not blossom, neither shall fruit be in the vines; the labour of the olive shall fail, and the fields shall yield no meat; the flock shall be cut off from the fold, and there shall be no herd in the stalls: yet I will rejoice in the LORD, I will joy in the God of my salvation.
HABAKKUK 3:17–18 KJV

Though the fig tree does not bud and there are no grapes on the vines, though the olive crop fails and the fields produce no food, though there are no sheep in the pen and no cattle in the stalls, yet I will rejoice in the LORD, I will be joyful in God my Savior.
HABAKKUK 3:17–18 NIV

How is it possible to have joy during such circumstances? You must love God and have a heart filled with gratitude for all He has done and all He will do—trusting Him during dark days to address any lack or injustice.

REJOICE, PRAY, AND BE THANKFUL

You may be baffled by Paul's instructions to "give thanks in *all* circumstances," especially when you're going through some horrid circumstances for which you're definitely not thankful. You may not even understand why you're expected to thank God for such things. But remember Job's reaction after the loss of all he owned: "The LORD gave and the LORD has taken away. Blessed be the name of the LORD" (Job 1:21 NASB).

Rejoice evermore. Pray without ceasing. In every thing give thanks: for this is the will of God in Christ Jesus concerning you.
1 THESSALONIANS 5:16–18 KJV

Rejoice always, pray continually, give thanks in all circumstances; for this is God's will for you in Christ Jesus.
1 THESSALONIANS 5:16–18 NIV

These verses have been divided into three separate thoughts in the KJV, but they actually are all part of one large thought in the NIV. You're not only to *give thanks* in all circumstances, but you are to *rejoice* in all circumstances and *pray* in all circumstances. Why? Because God is able to get good out of even evil situations (see Romans 8:28). Your job is to trust Him.

THE MEASURE YOU USE

Jesus promised that you would be blessed financially in proportion to how generously you gave. The word picture He used is that of pouring grain into a container and then stopping to press it down and shake the container so that the grain will settle and make room for more. God blesses you abundantly when you give.

Give, and it shall be given unto you; good measure, pressed down, and shaken together, and running over, shall men give into your bosom. For with the same measure that ye mete withal it shall be measured to you again.
LUKE 6:38 KJV

"Give, and it will be given to you. A good measure, pressed down, shaken together and running over, will be poured into your lap. For with the measure you use, it will be measured to you."
LUKE 6:38 NIV

This is one of God's principles: "With the measure you use, it will be measured to you." It also applies to how you treat others. Jesus said, "The standard you use in judging is the standard by which you will be judged" (Matthew 7:2 NLT).

LENDING AND GIVING FREELY

The verse below is well worth memorizing because, although it may be difficult to practice, let alone on an ongoing basis, it captures the heart of Jesus' message on giving. In a related passage, He said, "Give to everyone who asks you, and if anyone takes what belongs to you, do not demand it back" (Luke 6:30 NIV). The idea is that you're not to cling to your possessions.

Give to him that asketh thee, and from him that would borrow of thee turn not thou away.
MATTHEW 5:42 KJV

"Give to the one who asks you, and do not turn away from the one who wants to borrow from you."
MATTHEW 5:42 NIV

This principle was brought out in the Law of Moses. It says, "If there is a poor person among you. . .you shall not harden your heart, nor close your hand from your poor brother; but you shall fully open your hand to him, and generously lend him enough for his need" (Deuteronomy 15:7–8 NASB). Solomon added, "If you can help your neighbor now, don't say, 'Come back tomorrow, and then I'll help you'" (Proverbs 3:28 NLT).

HELPING THE DESPERATE

God's people are to work hard to supply their own needs. Paul said "that if any would not work, neither should he eat" (2 Thessalonians 3:10 KJV). Christians are not to be loafers, living off the labor of others. However, as far back as the Old Testament, God made provision for the fact that even hardworking individuals would fall on hard times and need emergency assistance. And God commanded His people to give generously to them (see Deuteronomy 15:10):

> *But whoso hath this world's good, and seeth his brother have need, and shutteth up his bowels of compassion from him, how dwelleth the love of God in him? My little children, let us not love in word, neither in tongue; but in deed and in truth.*
>
> 1 JOHN 3:17–18 KJV

> *If anyone has material possessions and sees a brother or sister in need but has no pity on them, how can the love of God be in that person? Dear children, let us not love with words or speech but with actions and in truth.*
>
> 1 JOHN 3:17–18 NIV

This passage applies to present-day followers of Christ as well.

MOTIVATIONS FOR TITHING

Many Christians believe that although the Old Testament Law is done away with in Christ (Hebrews 7:18; 10:9), the laws regarding tithing are still in effect. In the following verse, God has promised to bless those who give 10 percent of their income:

> *Bring ye all the tithes into the storehouse, that there may be meat in mine house, and prove me now herewith, saith the* L*ORD of hosts, if I will not open you the windows of heaven, and pour you out a blessing, that there shall not be room enough to receive it.*
>
> MALACHI 3:10 KJV

> *"Bring the whole tithe into the storehouse, that there may be food in my house. Test me in this," says the* L*ORD Almighty, "and see if I will not throw open the floodgates of heaven and pour out so much blessing that there will not be room enough to store it."*
>
> MALACHI 3:10 NIV

There are not only blessings for tithing, but—as it says in the verses preceding this—curses for those who fail to do so. Therefore, if tithing is still in effect in the age of grace, it's not an option or simply a path to blessing for those who so choose. It's a command.

CHRISTIAN GIVING

Throughout the Gospels, Jesus repeatedly urged His followers to give generously. The apostles likewise explained that God would bless those who give to support church workers and the needy (1 Corinthians 9:4–11; Ephesians 4:28). But they never told Christians to give a certain percentage of their income. They were simply to give what they felt they could—and to do so cheerfully.

Every man according as he purposeth in his heart,
so let him give; not grudgingly, or of necessity:
for God loveth a cheerful giver.
2 CORINTHIANS 9:7 KJV

Each of you should give what you have decided
in your heart to give, not reluctantly or under
compulsion, for God loves a cheerful giver.
2 CORINTHIANS 9:7 NIV

Paul urged believers to give generously, saying, "The one who sows sparingly will also reap sparingly, and the one who sows generously will also reap generously" (2 Corinthians 9:6 NASB). Rather than giving to avoid being cursed, the Christians living in the time of the apostles were motivated by anticipating degrees of blessing. It became standard practice for believers to give money every Sunday (see 1 Corinthians 16:2).

THE GREAT COMMISSION

This verse is often called "the Great Commission." A commission is "an instruction, command, or duty given to a person or group of people," and in this verse, Jesus commissioned His disciples to evangelize the whole world. In Acts 1:8 (NKJV) He said, "You shall be witnesses. . .to the end of the earth." He therefore commanded:

Go ye into all the world, and preach
the gospel to every creature.
MARK 16:15 KJV

"Go into all the world and preach
the gospel to all creation."
MARK 16:15 NIV

Once this command has been fulfilled, Jesus will return from the heavens to judge the world, reward His disciples, and set up His kingdom: "This gospel of the kingdom will be preached in all the world as a witness to all the nations, and then the end will come" (Matthew 24:14 NKJV). This prophecy is close to being fulfilled. The gospel is even now being preached in most of the world. But many nations remain tightly closed to Jesus' message, and many isolated people groups still need to hear the good news.

SHINING LIKE STARS

Describing Christians' future resurrected bodies, the apostle Paul compared them to the "glory of the stars" and noted that "one star differs from another star in glory" (1 Corinthians 15:41 NKJV). The verse below states that "they that turn many to righteousness" shall shine "as the stars for ever and ever." So God will definitely reward you for faithfully witnessing to the unsaved.

And they that be wise shall shine as the brightness of the firmament; and they that turn many to righteousness as the stars for ever and ever.
DANIEL 12:3 KJV

"Those who are wise will shine like the brightness of the heavens, and those who lead many to righteousness, like the stars for ever and ever."
DANIEL 12:3 NIV

Many Christians believe that they will receive "stars in their crown" for every soul won, and while there are hymns that declare this belief, it's not actually found in the Bible. The book of Daniel specifies that believers themselves shall shine like stars. The Greek myths stated that certain people and gods were transformed into constellations, but this will happen, in a sense, only to followers of Christ.

LET YOUR LIGHT SHINE

Jesus declared, "You are the light of the world. A city set on a hill cannot be hidden; nor do people light a lamp and put it under a basket, but on the lampstand, and it gives light to all who are in the house" (Matthew 5:14–15 NASB). God intends for your life to be a public witness to His grace and power working in you. You can be sure that people are watching you. Live with that knowledge.

Let your light so shine before men, that they may see your good works, and glorify your Father which is in heaven.
MATTHEW 5:16 KJV

"Let your light shine before others, that they may see your good deeds and glorify your Father in heaven."
MATTHEW 5:16 NIV

You're not saved by doing good works, but God fully intends that your life will be full of good works once He has saved you: "For we are His workmanship, created in Christ Jesus for good works, which God prepared beforehand so that we would walk in them" (Ephesians 2:10 NASB).

DISCIPLING THE NATIONS

The missionary David Livingstone often claimed the verse below when he was in danger. In it, Jesus states, "I am with you always, even unto the end of the world"—and in Livingstone's days, the jungles of Africa were as close to the "end of the world" as you could get. The NIV translates it "to the. . .end of the age," referring to a time rather than a location. Either way, Christians are to teach people all of Jesus' commands to the ends of the earth until the end of time.

Teaching them to observe all things whatsoever I have commanded you: and, lo, I am with you always, even unto the end of the world. Amen.
MATTHEW 28:20 KJV

"Teaching them to obey everything I have commanded you. And surely I am with you always, to the very end of the age."
MATTHEW 28:20 NIV

Jesus' most important command was to love God with all your heart and to love others as much as you love yourself—and if you seek to obey these two commands, you'll do very well because you'll then automatically obey all of Jesus' commands.

TEACHING THE WORD

All Christians are to teach the Word of God, even if not in a formal Bible study setting. After all, speaking of His commandments, God said, "You shall teach them diligently to your children, and shall talk of them when you sit in your house, when you walk by the way, when you lie down, and when you rise up" (Deuteronomy 6:7 NKJV). In other words, you are to teach the Word all the time. That's what the verse below means by "in season and out of season":

Preach the word; be instant in season,
out of season; reprove, rebuke, exhort with
all long suffering and doctrine.
2 TIMOTHY 4:2 KJV

Preach the word; be prepared in season and
out of season; correct, rebuke and encourage—
with great patience and careful instruction.
2 TIMOTHY 4:2 NIV

Instead of just correcting, rebuking, and encouraging someone with your own words, look for ways to weave God's Word into the conversation. It will give you authority. But to quote God's Word, you must first of all *know* it. And to know the Word, it helps to commit it to memory.

GODLINESS PROVOKES PERSECUTION

Living a godly lifestyle means refraining from evil activities, and the Bible teaches that this can bring on persecution: "You have had enough in the past of the evil things that godless people enjoy. . . . Of course, your former friends are surprised when you no longer plunge into the flood of wild and destructive things they do. So they slander you" (1 Peter 4:3–4 NLT). This shows that persecution doesn't always mean being spit on, beaten, or jailed. Often, persecution consists of slander, defamation, and insults. These alone can cause you grief and damage your reputation.

Yea, and all that will live godly in
Christ Jesus shall suffer persecution.
2 TIMOTHY 3:12 KJV

In fact, everyone who wants to live a godly
life in Christ Jesus will be persecuted.
2 TIMOTHY 3:12 NIV

No one really wants persecution, so why memorize such a discouraging promise? Because, as it says, you're guaranteed to suffer persecution if you choose to follow Christ. So it pays to be fully aware of this dynamic so that you aren't caught off guard when it happens. To be forewarned is to be forearmed.

DESTINED TO SUFFER

You may look at your life and the lives of Christians around you and wonder if the promise presented in the following verse actually applies. After all, you're probably not being violently persecuted for being a Christian. However, you may still be suffering. There could be ongoing arguments and tensions in your family because of your Christian faith. Also, there will be times when you're forced to take a stand and speak out on certain issues, and these views can make you unpopular.

For unto you it is given in the behalf of Christ,
not only to believe on him, but also to suffer for his sake.
PHILIPPIANS 1:29 KJV

For it has been granted to you on behalf of Christ not
only to believe in him, but also to suffer for him.
PHILIPPIANS 1:29 NIV

Jesus said, "If they persecuted Me, they will persecute you as well" (John 15:20 NASB). If you never have disagreements or differences of opinion with unbelievers, then the problem might be that you're not taking a clear stand for Christ. Remember that Jesus cautioned, "Woe to you when all people speak well of you" (Luke 6:26 NASB).

TEMPORARY POWER

Today your enemies may seem all-powerful. Their roots may appear to be locked deep in the soil, and their branches may form a thick canopy overhead. It seems they'll last forever, so you may feel like giving up. The British poet Shelley captured this in his poem *Ozymandias*, declaring, "My name is Ozymandias, king of kings: look on my works, ye Mighty, and despair!" But David declared:

> *I have seen the wicked in great power, and spreading himself like a green bay tree. Yet he passed away, and, lo, he was not: yea, I sought him, but he could not be found.*
> PSALM 37:35–36 KJV

> *I have seen a wicked and ruthless man flourishing like a luxuriant native tree, but he soon passed away and was no more; though I looked for him, he could not be found.*
> PSALM 37:35–36 NIV

Don't fret when the wicked are in power, when they threaten you and seek to work you woe. As King David also wrote, "For yet a little while, and the wicked shall not be: yea, thou shalt diligently consider his place, and it shall not be" (Psalm 37:10 KJV).

THE RETURN OF CHRIST

The following passage describes the rapture of Christians at Christ's second coming, when He takes us to heaven:

For the Lord himself shall descend from heaven with a shout, with the voice of the archangel, and with the trump of God: and the dead in Christ shall rise first: then we which are alive and remain shall be caught up together with them in the clouds, to meet the Lord in the air: and so shall we ever be with the Lord.

1 THESSALONIANS 4:16–17 KJV

For the Lord himself will come down from heaven, with a loud command, with the voice of the archangel and with the trumpet call of God, and the dead in Christ will rise first. After that, we who are still alive and are left will be caught up together with them in the clouds to meet the Lord in the air. And so we will be with the Lord forever.

1 THESSALONIANS 4:16–17 NIV

This passage ends by saying, "So encourage each other with these words" (verse 18 NLT). This is one of the main reasons to memorize this passage—to be able to encourage yourself and others.

RESURRECTED AND TRANSFORMED

All believers will be transformed at the rapture. The physical bodies of departed saints will be raised to life as powerful, supernatural bodies, and the physical bodies of those who are still alive in that day will be instantly changed. Our powerful new bodies will then live forever.

Behold, I shew you a mystery; We shall not all sleep, but we shall all be changed, in a moment, in the twinkling of an eye, at the last trump: for the trumpet shall sound, and the dead shall be raised incorruptible, and we shall be changed.
1 Corinthians 15:51–52 KJV

Listen, I tell you a mystery: We will not all sleep, but we will all be changed—in a flash, in the twinkling of an eye, at the last trumpet. For the trumpet will sound, the dead will be raised imperishable, and we will be changed.
1 Corinthians 15:51–52 NIV

God's children will have powers and abilities that they've never known before, and they will glow with great glory and beauty, like the angels of God. "We will be changed." What an encouraging promise!

JUDGMENT AFTER DEATH

The Bible teaches that there are *two* resurrections and two judgments. The first is "the resurrection of life" (John 5:29 KJV), which happens after the rapture when the saved appear before the "judgment seat of Christ" (2 Corinthians 5:10 KJV). There they're rewarded for their service. The second resurrection, "the resurrection of damnation," happens at the end of the millennium, when the unsaved appear at the great white throne judgment (Revelation 20:11–15). These two judgments are a thousand years apart.

And as it is appointed unto men once to die,
but after this the judgment: so Christ was
once offered to bear the sins of many.
HEBREWS 9:27–28 KJV

Just as people are destined to die once, and after
that to face judgment, so Christ was sacrificed
once to take away the sins of many.
HEBREWS 9:27–28 NIV

Just as Jesus only died once on the cross, all people on earth only die once. It's also good to quote this scripture to those who believe in reincarnation, which teaches that people undergo many births and deaths. The Bible states definitively that "people are destined to die once."

REAPING THE WHIRLWIND

One of Job's friends observed, "Those who plow iniquity and sow trouble reap the same" (Job 4:8 NKJV), and in the New Testament, Paul said that "whatever a man sows, that he will also reap" (Galatians 6:7 NKJV). In the following memory verse, the prophet Hosea described the Israelites who abandoned God to worship idols, and therefore faced judgment. Their land would be conquered by the cruel Assyrians; they would be deported to distant nations, be absorbed into those nations, and lose their distinct identity as a people.

For they have sown the wind, and they shall reap the whirlwind.
Hosea 8:7 KJV

"They sow the wind and reap the whirlwind."
Hosea 8:7 NIV

Why was their judgment on a greater magnitude than their sin? The plant that results is always greater than the seed sown. Know this: God was merciful even in judgment. Initially, He allowed many of the Israelites to stay in their land; only after they continued to rebel did the Assyrians first deport some of them, then finally deport them all (2 Kings 15:17–20, 27–29; 17:1–23). They could have easily avoided reaping the whirlwind.

WALKING TOGETHER

Paul wrote, "Do not be unequally yoked together with unbelievers. For what fellowship has righteousness with lawlessness?" (2 Corinthians 6:14 NKJV). Paul had Deuteronomy 22:10 (NKJV) in mind, which states, "You shall not plow with an ox and a donkey together." It's possible to bind these two animals together, but it only causes trouble—so the Law forbade it. For the same reason, you shouldn't bind yourself together with an unbeliever.

Can two walk together, except they be agreed?
AMOS 3:3 KJV

Do two walk together unless they have agreed to do so?
AMOS 3:3 NIV

On the other side of the coin, Christians all too often have difficulty working together with fellow believers. In today's memory verse, God points out that two travelers won't walk together unless they have agreed to do so. And they must remain in agreement, or they will soon cease walking together. Paul told the Philippians that he hoped to hear that they were standing "fast in one spirit, with one mind striving together for the faith of the gospel" (Philippians 1:27 NKJV).

GOD IS IN THE DETAILS

God asked, "Who hath despised the day of small things?" The answer is that at one time or another, most people have. You may disrespect small people because you think they're unimportant. You may disdain small beginnings because they don't seem to amount to much. You may overlook small details because they seem trivial. But God is in the details, and He works with the humble and the lowly (see 1 Corinthians 1:26–28). It's unwise to despise something that begins small, "for you do not know what a day may bring forth" (Proverbs 27:1 NKJV).

For who hath despised the day of small things?
ZECHARIAH 4:10 KJV

"Who dares despise the day of small things?"
ZECHARIAH 4:10 NIV

This short verse from Zechariah is worth memorizing as it helps you check your motives. Jesus said, "He that is faithful in that which is least is faithful also in much: and he that is unjust in the least is unjust also in much" (Luke 16:10 KJV).

8

LONGER PASSAGES AND CHAPTERS

If it seems like a daunting task to memorize an entire chapter, or even a passage several verses long, you can approach it an easier way. Don't attempt to memorize it. Rather, simply commit to faithfully read each of these passages once a week, and you'll find after a few months that you know them so well that you can practically quote them already. Then the Holy Spirit will be able to readily bring them to your remembrance when you need their message. You will also find that the constant reading will have prepared you to actually memorize the chapters—should you choose to do so at a later date.

The following chapters and passages have been chosen because of their powerful messages, but there may be other chapters that have special meanings for you. You may choose to memorize them as well.

Psalm 23

This psalm will comfort you when you're in danger or face great fear. Down through the ages, believers have quoted this short psalm and received great strength and encouragement. God's people have even quoted it when being tortured, and they found refuge.

1 The LORD is my shepherd; I shall not want. 2 He maketh me to lie down in green pastures: he leadeth me beside the still waters. 3 He restoreth my soul: he leadeth me in the paths of righteousness for his name's sake. 4 Yea, though I walk through the valley of the shadow of death, I will fear no evil: for thou art with me; thy rod and thy staff they comfort me. 5 Thou preparest a table before me in the presence of mine enemies: thou anointest my head with oil; my cup runneth over. 6 Surely goodness and mercy shall follow me all the days of my life: and I will dwell in the house of the LORD for ever.

PSALM 23 KJV

1 The LORD is my shepherd, I lack nothing. 2 He makes me lie down in green pastures, he leads me beside quiet waters, 3 he refreshes my soul. He guides me along the right paths for his name's sake. 4 Even though I walk through the darkest valley, I will fear no evil, for you are with me; your rod and your staff, they comfort me. 5 You prepare a table before me in the presence of my enemies. You anoint my head with oil; my cup overflows. 6 Surely your goodness and love will follow me all the days of my life, and I will dwell in the house of the LORD forever.

PSALM 23 NIV

Psalm 103:1–5, 8–14

This passage shows God's fatherly heart, and it reveals His intentions toward you.

[1]Bless the LORD, O my soul: and all that is within me, bless his holy
name. [2]Bless the LORD, O my soul, and forget not all his benefits:
[3]who forgiveth all thine iniquities; who healeth all thy diseases;
[4]who redeemeth thy life from destruction; who crowneth thee with
lovingkindness and tender mercies; [5]who satisfieth thy mouth with
good things; so that thy youth is renewed like the eagle's. . . . [8]The LORD
is merciful and gracious, slow to anger, and plenteous in mercy. [9]He
will not always chide: neither will he keep his anger for ever. [10]He
hath not dealt with us after our sins; nor rewarded us according to
our iniquities. [11]For as the heaven is high above the earth, so great
is his mercy toward them that fear him. [12]As far as the east is from
the west, so far hath he removed our transgressions from us. [13]Like
as a father pitieth his children, so the LORD pitieth them that fear
him. [14]For he knoweth our frame; he remembereth that we are dust.

PSALM 103:1–5, 8–14 KJV

[1]Praise the LORD, my soul; all my inmost being, praise his holy name.
[2]Praise the LORD, my soul, and forget not all his benefits— [3]who
forgives all your sins and heals all your diseases, [4]who redeems your
life from the pit and crowns you with love and compassion, [5]who
satisfies your desires with good things so that your youth is renewed
like the eagle's. . . . [8]The LORD is compassionate and gracious,
slow to anger, abounding in love. [9]He will not always accuse, nor
will he harbor his anger forever; [10]he does not treat us as our sins
deserve or repay us according to our iniquities. [11]For as high as the
heavens are above the earth, so great is his love for those who fear
him; [12]as far as the east is from the west, so far has he removed

our transgressions from us. [13]*As a father has compassion on his children, so the* LORD *has compassion on those who fear him;* [14]*for he knows how we are formed, he remembers that we are dust.*
PSALM 103:1–5, 8–14 NIV

Isaiah 53

Isaiah gave the prophecies in this chapter six hundred years before the birth of Jesus, and they were amazingly fulfilled in His trial, death, and burial. Isaiah 53 explains in unmistakable terms that the Jewish Messiah would die for the sins of His people.

The book of Isaiah was found among the Dead Sea Scrolls, and this chapter was identical in almost all details to the text found in the ancient scroll of Isaiah, proving that this prophecy was the same before the birth of Christ. This is proof that the church didn't doctor the Old Testament prophecies to make them look like Jesus had fulfilled them. He really was the Messiah, and He really did die for the sins of humanity.

[1]*Who hath believed our report? and to whom is the arm of the* LORD
revealed? [2]*For he shall grow up before him as a tender plant, and as*
a root out of a dry ground: he hath no form nor comeliness; and when
we shall see him, there is no beauty that we should desire him. [3]*He is*
despised and rejected of men; a man of sorrows, and acquainted with
grief: and we hid as it were our faces from him; he was despised, and
we esteemed him not. [4]*Surely he hath borne our griefs, and carried our*
sorrows: yet we did esteem him stricken, smitten of God, and afflicted.
[5]*But he was wounded for our transgressions, he was bruised for our*
iniquities: the chastisement of our peace was upon him; and with his
stripes we are healed. [6]*All we like sheep have gone astray; we have*
turned every one to his own way; and the LORD *hath laid on him*

the iniquity of us all. 7*He was oppressed, and he was afflicted, yet he*
opened not his mouth: he is brought as a lamb to the slaughter, and as
a sheep before her shearers is dumb, so he openeth not his mouth. 8*He*
was taken from prison and from judgment: and who shall declare
his generation? for he was cut off out of the land of the living: for the
transgression of my people was he stricken. 9*And he made his grave*
with the wicked, and with the rich in his death; because he had done
no violence, neither was any deceit in his mouth. 10*Yet it pleased the*
LORD to bruise him; he hath put him to grief: when thou shalt make his
soul an offering for sin, he shall see his seed, he shall prolong his days,
and the pleasure of the LORD shall prosper in his hand. 11*He shall see*
of the travail of his soul, and shall be satisfied: by his knowledge shall
my righteous servant justify many; for he shall bear their iniquities.
12*Therefore will I divide him a portion with the great, and he shall*
divide the spoil with the strong; because he hath poured out his soul
unto death: and he was numbered with the transgressors; and he
bare the sin of many, and made intercession for the transgressors.

ISAIAH 53 KJV

1*Who has believed our message and to whom has the arm of*
the LORD been revealed? 2*He grew up before him like a tender*
shoot, and like a root out of dry ground. He had no beauty or
majesty to attract us to him, nothing in his appearance that we
should desire him. 3*He was despised and rejected by mankind, a*
man of suffering, and familiar with pain. Like one from whom
people hide their faces he was despised, and we held him in
low esteem. 4*Surely he took up our pain and bore our suffering,*
yet we considered him punished by God, stricken by him,
and afflicted. 5*But he was pierced for our transgressions, he was*
crushed for our iniquities; the punishment that brought us peace was
on him, and by his wounds we are healed. 6*We all, like sheep, have*

gone astray, each of us has turned to our own way; and the LORD has
laid on him the iniquity of us all. [7]He was oppressed and afflicted, yet
he did not open his mouth; he was led like a lamb to the slaughter, and
as a sheep before its shearers is silent, so he did not open his mouth.
[8]By oppression and judgment he was taken away. Yet who of his
generation protested? For he was cut off from the land of the living;
for the transgression of my people he was punished. [9]He was assigned
a grave with the wicked, and with the rich in his death, though he
had done no violence, nor was any deceit in his mouth. [10]Yet it was
the LORD's will to crush him and cause him to suffer, and though the
LORD makes his life an offering for sin, he will see his offspring and
prolong his days, and the will of the LORD will prosper in his hand.
[11]After he has suffered, he will see the light of life and be satisfied; by
his knowledge my righteous servant will justify many, and he will
bear their iniquities. [12]Therefore I will give him a portion among the
great, and he will divide the spoils with the strong, because he poured
out his life unto death, and was numbered with the transgressors. For
he bore the sin of many, and made intercession for the transgressors.

ISAIAH 53 NIV

John 1:1–14

The following preface to the Gospel of John boldly declares the deity of Christ. John's Gospel repeatedly mentions that Jesus is one with God His Father, and John stated it up front to make sure you couldn't miss the point.

> *1 In the beginning was the Word, and the Word was with God,*
> *and the Word was God. 2 The same was in the beginning with*
> *God. 3 All things were made by him; and without him was not*
> *any thing made that was made. 4 In him was life; and the life was*
> *the light of men. 5 And the light shineth in darkness; and the darkness*
> *comprehended it not. 6 There was a man sent from God, whose name*
> *was John. 7 The same came for a witness, to bear witness of the Light,*
> *that all men through him might believe. 8 He was not that Light, but*
> *was sent to bear witness of that Light. 9 That was the true Light, which*
> *lighteth every man that cometh into the world. 10 He was in the world,*
> *and the world was made by him, and the world knew him not. 11 He*
> *came unto his own, and his own received him not. 12 But as many as*
> *received him, to them gave he power to become the sons of God, even*
> *to them that believe on his name: 13 which were born, not of blood, nor*
> *of the will of the flesh, nor of the will of man, but of God. 14 And the*
> *Word was made flesh, and dwelt among us, (and we beheld his glory,*
> *the glory as of the only begotten of the Father,) full of grace and truth.*
>
> JOHN 1:1–14 KJV

> *1 In the beginning was the Word, and the Word was with God, and the*
> *Word was God. 2 He was with God in the beginning. 3 Through him all*
> *things were made; without him nothing was made that has been made.*
> *4 In him was life, and that life was the light of all mankind. 5 The light*
> *shines in the darkness, and the darkness has not overcome it. 6 There was*
> *a man sent from God whose name was John. 7 He came as a witness to*

testify concerning that light, so that through him all might believe.
8He himself was not the light; he came only as a witness to the light.
9The true light that gives light to everyone was coming into the world.
10He was in the world, and though the world was made through him,
the world did not recognize him. 11He came to that which was his own,
but his own did not receive him. 12Yet to all who did receive him, to
those who believed in his name, he gave the right to become children of
God— 13children born not of natural descent, nor of human decision
or a husband's will, but born of God. 14The Word became flesh and
made his dwelling among us. We have seen his glory, the glory of the
one and only Son, who came from the Father, full of grace and truth.

JOHN 1:1–14 NIV

John 15:1–8

This passage gives the secret to having spiritual strength and to accomplishing things for God. Memorizing this passage can greatly encourage you and strengthen your faith.

1I am the true vine, and my Father is the husbandman. 2Every
branch in me that beareth not fruit he taketh away: and every branch
that beareth fruit, he purgeth it, that it may bring forth more fruit.
3Now ye are clean through the word which I have spoken unto you.
4Abide in me, and I in you. As the branch cannot bear fruit of itself,
except it abide in the vine; no more can ye, except ye abide in me.
5I am the vine, ye are the branches: He that abideth in me, and I in
him, the same bringeth forth much fruit: for without me ye can do
nothing. 6If a man abide not in me, he is cast forth as a branch, and
is withered; and men gather them, and cast them into the fire, and
they are burned. 7If ye abide in me, and my words abide in you, ye
shall ask what ye will, and it shall be done unto you. 8Herein is my
Father glorified, that ye bear much fruit; so shall ye be my disciples.

JOHN 15:1–8 KJV

1“I am the true vine, and my Father is the gardener. 2He cuts off every
branch in me that bears no fruit, while every branch that does bear
fruit he prunes so that it will be even more fruitful. 3You are already
clean because of the word I have spoken to you. 4Remain in me, as I
also remain in you. No branch can bear fruit by itself; it must remain
in the vine. Neither can you bear fruit unless you remain in me. 5I
am the vine; you are the branches. If you remain in me and I in you,
you will bear much fruit; apart from me you can do nothing. 6If you
do not remain in me, you are like a branch that is thrown away and
withers; such branches are picked up, thrown into the fire and burned.
7If you remain in me and my words remain in you, ask whatever
you wish, and it will be done for you. 8This is to my Father's glory,
that you bear much fruit, showing yourselves to be my disciples.”

John 15:1–8 NIV

1 Corinthians 3:11–15

This passage proves that even though you haven't always lived as faithfully for Christ as you ought to, your salvation in Him is secure.

11For other foundation can no man lay than that is laid, which is
Jesus Christ. 12Now if any man build upon this foundation gold,
silver, precious stones, wood, hay, stubble; 13every man's work shall
be made manifest: for the day shall declare it, because it shall be
revealed by fire; and the fire shall try every man's work of what
sort it is. 14If any man's work abide which he hath built thereupon,
he shall receive a reward. 15If any man's work shall be burned, he
shall suffer loss: but he himself shall be saved; yet so as by fire.

1 Corinthians 3:11–15 KJV

11 For no one can lay any foundation other than the one already laid,
which is Jesus Christ. 12 If anyone builds on this foundation using
gold, silver, costly stones, wood, hay or straw, 13 their work will be
shown for what it is, because the Day will bring it to light. It will
be revealed with fire, and the fire will test the quality of each person's
work. 14 If what has been built survives, the builder will receive a
reward. 15 If it is burned up, the builder will suffer loss but yet will
be saved—even though only as one escaping through the flames.

1 CORINTHIANS 3:11–15 NIV

1 Corinthians 13

If you memorize this chapter in the King James Version, you may wonder what to do with the word *charity*. Four hundred years ago, "charity" meant altruistic love; these days, it chiefly means alms given to the poor. So even though you love the KJV, don't hesitate to substitute "love" in place of "charity" when quoting this.

This chapter is very important because it lets you know the kind of love God expects of you as a believer. First John 4:7–8, 16 (NIV) says that you know you're saved ("born of God. . .knows God. . .God is love") if you have love. And this is the kind of love it's referring to.

1 Though I speak with the tongues of men and of angels, and have
not charity, I am become as sounding brass, or a tinkling cymbal.
2 And though I have the gift of prophecy, and understand
all mysteries, and all knowledge; and though I have all faith, so
that I could remove mountains, and have not charity, I am nothing.
3 And though I bestow all my goods to feed the poor, and though I
give my body to be burned, and have not charity, it profiteth me
nothing. 4 Charity suffereth long, and is kind; charity envieth not;

charity vaunteth not itself, is not puffed up, [5]*doth not behave itself*
unseemly, seeketh not her own, is not easily provoked, thinketh no
evil; [6]*rejoiceth not in iniquity, but rejoiceth in the truth;* [7]*beareth all*
things, believeth all things, hopeth all things, endureth all things.
[8]*Charity never faileth: but whether there be prophecies, they shall*
fail; whether there be tongues, they shall cease; whether there be
knowledge, it shall vanish away. [9]*For we know in part, and we*
prophesy in part. [10]*But when that which is perfect is come, then*
that which is in part shall be done away. [11]*When I was a child, I*
spake as a child, I understood as a child, I thought as a child: but
when I became a man, I put away childish things. [12]*For now we see*
through a glass, darkly; but then face to face: now I know in part;
but then shall I know even as also I am known. [13]*And now abideth*
faith, hope, charity, these three; but the greatest of these is charity.

1 CORINTHIANS 13 KJV

[1]*If I speak in the tongues of men or of angels, but do not have love,*
I am only a resounding gong or a clanging cymbal. [2]*If I have the gift*
of prophecy and can fathom all mysteries and all knowledge, and if
I have a faith that can move mountains, but do not have love, I am
nothing. [3]*If I give all I possess to the poor and give over my body*
to hardship that I may boast, but do not have love, I gain nothing.
[4]*Love is patient, love is kind. It does not envy, it does not boast, it is*
not proud. [5]*It does not dishonor others, it is not self-seeking, it is not*
easily angered, it keeps no record of wrongs. [6]*Love does not delight*
in evil but rejoices with the truth. [7]*It always protects, always trusts,*
always hopes, always perseveres. [8]*Love never fails. But where there*
are prophecies, they will cease; where there are tongues, they will be
stilled; where there is knowledge, it will pass away. [9]*For we know in*
part and we prophesy in part, [10]*but when completeness comes, what*
is in part disappears. [11]*When I was a child, I talked like a child,*

I thought like a child, I reasoned like a child. When I became a man, I put the ways of childhood behind me. [12]*For now we see only a reflection as in a mirror; then we shall see face to face. Now I know in part; then I shall know fully, even as I am fully known.* [13]*And now these three remain: faith, hope and love. But the greatest of these is love.*

1 Corinthians 13 NIV

Ephesians 6:10–17

This is a favorite memory project for many Christians, as it describes how to protect yourself spiritually and to fight to defend the truth.

[10]*Finally, my brethren, be strong in the Lord, and in the power*
of his might. [11]*Put on the whole armour of God, that ye may be*
able to stand against the wiles of the devil. [12]*For we wrestle not*
against flesh and blood, but against principalities, against powers,
against the rulers of the darkness of this world, against spiritual
wickedness in high places. [13]*Wherefore take unto you the whole*
armour of God, that ye may be able to withstand in the evil day, and
having done all, to stand. [14]*Stand therefore, having your loins girt*
about with truth, and having on the breastplate of righteousness;
[15]*and your feet shod with the preparation of the gospel of peace;*
[16]*above all, taking the shield of faith, wherewith ye shall be able*
to quench all the fiery darts of the wicked. [17]*And take the helmet of*
salvation, and the sword of the Spirit, which is the word of God.

Ephesians 6:10–17 KJV

10 Finally, be strong in the Lord and in his mighty power. 11 Put on the full armor of God, so that you can take your stand against the devil's schemes. 12 For our struggle is not against flesh and blood, but against the rulers, against the authorities, against the powers of this dark world and against the spiritual forces of evil in the heavenly realms. 13 Therefore put on the full armor of God, so that when the day of evil comes, you may be able to stand your ground, and after you have done everything, to stand. 14 Stand firm then, with the belt of truth buckled around your waist, with the breastplate of righteousness in place, 15 and with your feet fitted with the readiness that comes from the gospel of peace. 16 In addition to all this, take up the shield of faith, with which you can extinguish all the flaming arrows of the evil one. 17 Take the helmet of salvation and the sword of the Spirit, which is the word of God.

Ephesians 6:10–17 NIV

Hebrews 12:1–11

This passage, if you will commit to memorizing it, will encourage you during many difficult seasons in your life when you're surrounded by hardships and tempted to doubt that the Lord loves you. He never stops loving you! In fact, the difficulties you face are often sure proof that God loves you and hasn't given up on you.

1 Wherefore seeing we also are compassed about with so great a cloud of witnesses, let us lay aside every weight, and the sin which doth so easily beset us, and let us run with patience the race that is set before us, 2 looking unto Jesus the author and finisher of our faith; who for the joy that was set before him endured the cross, despising the shame, and is set down at the right hand of the throne of God. 3 For consider him that endured such contradiction of sinners against himself, lest ye be wearied

and faint in your minds. 4Ye have not yet resisted unto blood, striving
against sin. 5And ye have forgotten the exhortation which speaketh
unto you as unto children, My son, despise not thou the chastening
of the Lord, nor faint when thou art rebuked of him: 6for whom the
Lord loveth he chasteneth, and scourgeth every son whom he receiveth.
7If ye endure chastening, God dealeth with you as with sons; for
what son is he whom the father chasteneth not? 8But if ye be without
chastisement, whereof all are partakers, then are ye bastards, and not
sons. 9Furthermore we have had fathers of our flesh which corrected us,
and we gave them reverence: shall we not much rather be in subjection
unto the Father of spirits, and live? 10For they verily for a few days
chastened us after their own pleasure; but he for our profit, that we
might be partakers of his holiness. 11Now no chastening for the present
seemeth to be joyous, but grievous: nevertheless afterward it yieldeth the
peaceable fruit of righteousness unto them which are exercised thereby.
HEBREWS 12:1–11 KJV

1Therefore, since we are surrounded by such a great cloud of witnesses,
let us throw off everything that hinders and the sin that so easily
entangles. And let us run with perseverance the race marked out
for us, 2fixing our eyes on Jesus, the pioneer and perfecter of faith.
For the joy set before him he endured the cross, scorning its shame,
and sat down at the right hand of the throne of God. 3Consider
him who endured such opposition from sinners, so that you will
not grow weary and lose heart. 4In your struggle against sin, you
have not yet resisted to the point of shedding your blood. 5And have
you completely forgotten this word of encouragement that addresses
you as a father addresses his son? It says, "My son, do not make
light of the Lord's discipline, and do not lose heart when he rebukes
you, 6because the Lord disciplines the one he loves, and he chastens
everyone he accepts as his son." 7Endure hardship as discipline; God

is treating you as his children. For what children are not disciplined by their father? [8]If you are not disciplined—and everyone undergoes discipline—then you are not legitimate, not true sons and daughters at all. [9]Moreover, we have all had human fathers who disciplined us and we respected them for it. How much more should we submit to the Father of spirits and live! [10]They disciplined us for a little while as they thought best; but God disciplines us for our good, in order that we may share in his holiness. [11]No discipline seems pleasant at the time, but painful. Later on, however, it produces a harvest of righteousness and peace for those who have been trained by it.

Hebrews 12:1–11 NIV

9

ADDITIONAL MEMORY VERSES

Salvation

Jesus answered and said unto him, Verily, verily, I say unto thee, Except a man be born again, he cannot see the kingdom of God.
JOHN 3:3 KJV

Jesus replied, "Very truly I tell you, no one can see the kingdom of God unless they are born again."
JOHN 3:3 NIV

Salvation

He that believeth on the Son hath everlasting life: and he that believeth not the Son shall not see life; but the wrath of God abideth on him.
JOHN 3:36 KJV

Whoever believes in the Son has eternal life, but whoever rejects the Son will not see life, for God's wrath remains on them.
JOHN 3:36 NIV

Salvation

Not by works of righteousness which we have done, but according to his mercy he saved us, by the washing of regeneration, and renewing of the Holy Ghost.

Titus 3:5 KJV

He saved us, not because of righteous things we had done, but because of his mercy. He saved us through the washing of rebirth and renewal by the Holy Spirit.

Titus 3:5 NIV

God Keeps You

Now he which stablisheth us with you in Christ, and hath anointed us, is God; who hath also sealed us, and given the earnest of the Spirit in our hearts.

2 Corinthians 1:21–22 KJV

Now it is God who makes both us and you stand firm in Christ. He anointed us, set his seal of ownership on us, and put his Spirit in our hearts as a deposit, guaranteeing what is to come.

2 Corinthians 1:21–22 NIV

God Keeps You

I know whom I have believed, and am persuaded that he is able to keep that which I have committed unto him against that day.

2 Timothy 1:12 KJV

I know whom I have believed, and am convinced that he is able to guard what I have entrusted to him until that day.
2 Timothy 1:12 NIV

God's Mercy

O my God, incline thine ear, and hear. . .for we do not present our supplications before thee for our righteousnesses, but for thy great mercies.
Daniel 9:18 KJV

"Give ear, our God, and hear. . . . We do not make requests of you because we are righteous, but because of your great mercy."
Daniel 9:18 NIV

Holy Spirit

And we are his witnesses of these things; and so is also the Holy Ghost, whom God hath given to them that obey him.
Acts 5:32 KJV

"We are witnesses of these things, and so is the Holy Spirit, whom God has given to those who obey him."
Acts 5:32 NIV

Growing Spiritually

But we all, with open face beholding as in a glass the glory of the Lord, are changed into the same image from glory to glory, even as by the Spirit of the Lord.
2 Corinthians 3:18 KJV

And we all, who with unveiled faces contemplate the Lord's glory, are being transformed into his image with ever-increasing glory, which comes from the Lord, who is the Spirit.

2 Corinthians 3:18 NIV

Growing Spiritually

As newborn babes, desire the sincere milk of the word, that ye may grow thereby.

1 Peter 2:2 KJV

Like newborn babies, crave pure spiritual milk, so that by it you may grow up in your salvation.

1 Peter 2:2 NIV

Growing Spiritually

As ye have therefore received Christ Jesus the Lord, so walk ye in him: rooted and built up in him, and stablished in the faith, as ye have been taught, abounding therein with thanksgiving.

Colossians 2:6–7 KJV

So then, just as you received Christ Jesus as Lord, continue to live your lives in him, rooted and built up in him, strengthened in the faith as you were taught, and overflowing with thankfulness.

Colossians 2:6–7 NIV

Abiding in Christ

Whosoever transgresseth, and abideth not in the doctrine of Christ, hath not God. He that abideth in the doctrine of Christ, he hath both the Father and the Son.

2 John 9 KJV

Anyone who runs ahead and does not continue in the teaching of Christ does not have God; whoever continues in the teaching has both the Father and the Son.

2 John 9 NIV

Loving Others

This is my commandment,
That ye love one another, as I have loved you.

John 15:12 KJV

"My command is this: Love each other as I have loved you."

John 15:12 NIV

Discipleship

Ye have heard that it hath been said, An eye for an eye, and a tooth for a tooth: but I say unto you, That ye resist not evil: but whosoever shall smite thee on thy right cheek, turn to him the other also.

Matthew 5:38–39 KJV

"You have heard that it was said, 'Eye for eye, and tooth for tooth.' But I tell you, do not resist an evil person. If anyone slaps you on the right cheek, turn to them the other cheek also."

Matthew 5:38–39 NIV

Discipleship

I have no greater joy than to hear that my children walk in truth.
3 John 4 KJV

I have no greater joy than to hear that my children are walking in the truth.
3 John 4 NIV

Word of God

Study to shew thyself approved unto God, a workman that needeth not to be ashamed, rightly dividing the word of truth.
2 Timothy 2:15 KJV

Do your best to present yourself to God as one approved, a worker who does not need to be ashamed and who correctly handles the word of truth.
2 Timothy 2:15 NIV

Unbelief

The fool hath said in his heart, There is no God.
Psalm 14:1 KJV

The fool says in his heart, "There is no God."
Psalm 14:1 NIV

Trust

Ye shall not need to fight in this battle: set yourselves,
stand ye still, and see the salvation of the LORD with you.
2 CHRONICLES 20:17 KJV

"You will not have to fight this battle. Take up your positions;
stand firm and see the deliverance the LORD will give you."
2 CHRONICLES 20:17 NIV

Trust

Commit thy works unto the LORD,
and thy thoughts shall be established.
PROVERBS 16:3 KJV

Commit to the LORD whatever you do,
and he will establish your plans.
PROVERBS 16:3 NIV

Trust

Thus saith the LORD; Cursed be the man that trusteth in man,
and maketh flesh his arm, and whose heart departeth from the LORD.
JEREMIAH 17:5 KJV

This is what the LORD says: "Cursed is the one who
trusts in man, who draws strength from mere flesh
and whose heart turns away from the LORD."
JEREMIAH 17:5 NIV

Suffering

But the God of all grace, who hath called us unto his eternal glory by Christ Jesus, after that ye have suffered a while, make you perfect, stablish, strengthen, settle you.
1 PETER 5:10 KJV

And the God of all grace, who called you to his eternal glory in Christ, after you have suffered a little while, will himself restore you and make you strong, firm and steadfast.
1 PETER 5:10 NIV

Chastisement

O LORD, correct me, but with judgment;
not in thine anger, lest thou bring me to nothing.
JEREMIAH 10:24 KJV

Discipline me, LORD, but only in due measure—
not in your anger, or you will reduce me to nothing.
JEREMIAH 10:24 NIV

God's Attributes

God is a Spirit: and they that worship him must worship him in spirit and in truth.
JOHN 4:24 KJV

"God is spirit, and his worshipers must worship in the Spirit and in truth."
JOHN 4:24 NIV

God's Attributes

I knew that thou art a gracious God, and merciful, slow to anger, and of great kindness, and repentest thee of the evil.
JONAH 4:2 KJV

"I knew that you are a gracious and compassionate God, slow to anger and abounding in love, a God who relents from sending calamity."
JONAH 4:2 NIV

Wisdom

The wise men are ashamed, they are dismayed and taken: lo, they have rejected the word of the LORD; and what wisdom is in them?
JEREMIAH 8:9 KJV

"The wise will be put to shame; they will be dismayed and trapped. Since they have rejected the word of the LORD, what kind of wisdom do they have?"
JEREMIAH 8:9 NIV

Wisdom

Behold, I send you forth as sheep in the midst of wolves: be ye therefore wise as serpents, and harmless as doves.
MATTHEW 10:16 KJV

"I am sending you out like sheep among wolves. Therefore be as shrewd as snakes and as innocent as doves."
MATTHEW 10:16 NIV

Guidance

When my spirit was overwhelmed within me, then thou knewest my path.
PSALM 142:3 KJV

When my spirit grows faint within me, it is you who watch over my way.
PSALM 142:3 NIV

Protection

No weapon that is formed against thee shall prosper; and every tongue that shall rise against thee in judgment thou shalt condemn. This is the heritage of the servants of the LORD, and their righteousness is of me, saith the LORD.
ISAIAH 54:17 KJV

"No weapon forged against you will prevail, and you will refute every tongue that accuses you. This is the heritage of the servants of the LORD, and this is their vindication from me," declares the LORD.
ISAIAH 54:17 NIV

Power

With men it is impossible, but not with God: for with God all things are possible.
MARK 10:27 KJV

"With man this is impossible, but not with God; all things are possible with God."
MARK 10:27 NIV

Power

He giveth power to the faint; and to them that have no might he increaseth strength. Even the youths shall faint and be weary, and the young men shall utterly fall: but they that wait upon the Lord *shall renew their strength; they shall mount up with wings as eagles; they shall run, and not be weary; and they shall walk, and not faint.*

Isaiah 40:29–31 kjv

He gives strength to the weary and increases the power of the weak. Even youths grow tired and weary, and young men stumble and fall; but those who hope in the Lord *will renew their strength. They will soar on wings like eagles; they will run and not grow weary, they will walk and not be faint.*

Isaiah 40:29–31 niv

Overcoming Evil

How God anointed Jesus of Nazareth with the Holy Ghost and with power: who went about doing good, and healing all that were oppressed of the devil; for God was with him.

Acts 10:38 kjv

"How God anointed Jesus of Nazareth with the Holy Spirit and power, and how he went around doing good and healing all who were under the power of the devil, because God was with him."

Acts 10:38 niv

God's Promises

For the vision is yet for an appointed time, but at the end it shall speak, and not lie: though it tarry, wait for it; because it will surely come, it will not tarry.

Habakkuk 2:3 KJV

"For the revelation awaits an appointed time; it speaks of the end and will not prove false. Though it linger, wait for it; it will certainly come and will not delay."

Habakkuk 2:3 NIV

God's Promises

The Lord thy God in the midst of thee is mighty; he will save, he will rejoice over thee with joy; he will rest in his love, he will joy over thee with singing.

Zephaniah 3:17 KJV

"The Lord your God is with you, the Mighty Warrior who saves. He will take great delight in you; in his love he will no longer rebuke you, but will rejoice over you with singing."

Zephaniah 3:17 NIV

Witnessing

For the preaching of the cross is to them that perish foolishness; but unto us which are saved it is the power of God.

1 Corinthians 1:18 KJV

For the message of the cross is foolishness to those who are perishing, but to us who are being saved it is the power of God.
1 Corinthians 1:18 NIV

Healing

If thou wilt diligently hearken to the voice of the Lord thy God, and wilt do that which is right in his sight, and wilt give ear to his commandments, and keep all his statutes, I will put none of these diseases upon thee, which I have brought upon the Egyptians: for I am the Lord that healeth thee.
Exodus 15:26 KJV

"If you listen carefully to the Lord your God and do what is right in his eyes, if you pay attention to his commands and keep all his decrees, I will not bring on you any of the diseases I brought on the Egyptians, for I am the Lord, who heals you."
Exodus 15:26 NIV

Healing

Is any sick among you? let him call for the elders of the church; and let them pray over him, anointing him with oil in the name of the Lord: and the prayer of faith shall save the sick, and the Lord shall raise him up; and if he have committed sins, they shall be forgiven him. Confess your faults one to another, and pray one for another, that ye may be healed. The effectual fervent prayer of a righteous man availeth much.
James 5:14–16 KJV

Is anyone among you sick? Let them call the elders of the church to pray over them and anoint them with oil in the name of the Lord. And the prayer offered in faith will make the sick person well; the Lord will raise them up. If they have sinned, they will be forgiven. Therefore confess your sins to each other and pray for each other so that you may be healed. The prayer of a righteous person is powerful and effective.

JAMES 5:14–16 NIV

Healing

But unto you that fear my name shall the Sun of righteousness arise with healing in his wings.

MALACHI 4:2 KJV

"But for you who revere my name, the sun of righteousness will rise with healing in its rays."

MALACHI 4:2 NIV

Fear of God

And fear not them which kill the body, but are not able to kill the soul: but rather fear him which is able to destroy both soul and body in hell.

MATTHEW 10:28 KJV

"Do not be afraid of those who kill the body but cannot kill the soul. Rather, be afraid of the One who can destroy both soul and body in hell."

MATTHEW 10:28 NIV

Creation

The heavens declare the glory of God;
and the firmament sheweth his handywork.
PSALM 19:1 KJV

The heavens declare the glory of God;
the skies proclaim the work of his hands.
PSALM 19:1 NIV

Creation

He hath made the earth by his power, he hath established the world by his wisdom, and hath stretched out the heaven by his understanding.
JEREMIAH 51:15 KJV

"He made the earth by his power; he founded the world by his wisdom and stretched out the heavens by his understanding."
JEREMIAH 51:15 NIV

Purity

Wherewithal shall a young man cleanse his way?
by taking heed thereto according to thy word.
PSALM 119:9 KJV

How can a young person stay on the path of purity? By living according to your word.
PSALM 119:9 NIV

Sin

Behold, the LORD's hand is not shortened, that it cannot save; neither his ear heavy, that it cannot hear: but your iniquities have separated between you and your God, and your sins have hid his face from you, that he will not hear.
ISAIAH 59:1–2 KJV

Surely the arm of the LORD is not too short to save, nor his ear too dull to hear. But your iniquities have separated you from your God; your sins have hidden his face from you, so that he will not hear.
ISAIAH 59:1–2 NIV

Sin

Take us the foxes, the little foxes, that spoil the vines.
SONG OF SOLOMON 2:15 KJV

Catch for us the foxes, the little foxes that ruin the vineyards.
SONG OF SONGS 2:15 NIV

Sin

The heart is deceitful above all things,
and desperately wicked: who can know it?
JEREMIAH 17:9 KJV

The heart is deceitful above all things and
beyond cure. Who can understand it?
JEREMIAH 17:9 NIV

Sin

Ye have sown much, and bring in little; ye eat, but ye have not enough; ye drink, but ye are not filled with drink; ye clothe you, but there is none warm; and he that earneth wages earneth wages to put it into a bag with holes.
HAGGAI 1:6 KJV

"You have planted much, but harvested little. You eat, but never have enough. You drink, but never have your fill. You put on clothes, but are not warm. You earn wages, only to put them in a purse with holes in it."
HAGGAI 1:6 NIV

Pride

Though thou exalt thyself as the eagle, and though thou set thy nest among the stars, thence will I bring thee down, saith the LORD.
OBADIAH 4 KJV

"Though you soar like the eagle and make your nest among the stars, from there I will bring you down," declares the LORD.
OBADIAH 4 NIV

Hope

Seeing then that we have such hope, we use great plainness of speech.
2 CORINTHIANS 3:12 KJV

Therefore, since we have such a hope, we are very bold.
2 CORINTHIANS 3:12 NIV

Repentance

And I sought for a man among them, that should make up the hedge, and stand in the gap before me for the land, that I should not destroy it: but I found none.
EZEKIEL 22:30 KJV

"I looked for someone among them who would build up the wall and stand before me in the gap on behalf of the land so I would not have to destroy it, but I found no one."
EZEKIEL 22:30 NIV

God's Provision

But thou shalt remember the LORD thy God: for it is he that giveth thee power to get wealth.
DEUTERONOMY 8:18 KJV

But remember the LORD your God, for it is he who gives you the ability to produce wealth.
DEUTERONOMY 8:18 NIV

Diligence

He that is faithful in that which is least is faithful also in much: and he that is unjust in the least is unjust also in much.
LUKE 16:10 KJV

"Whoever can be trusted with very little can also be trusted with much, and whoever is dishonest with very little will also be dishonest with much."
LUKE 16:10 NIV

144 MEMORY VERSES INDEX

ADDITIONAL MEMORY VERSES INDEX

TOPICAL INDEX